Grampy's War

Colin Simmons

Copyright © Colin Simmons 2009

This work is based on the tapes of Frederick Britt as transcribed and edited by Colin Simmons

All rights reserved. No part of this book may be reproduced, stored, or transmitted by any means—whether auditory, graphic, mechanical, or electronic—without written permission of both publisher and author, except in the case of brief excerpts used in critical articles and reviews. Unauthorized reproduction of any part of this work is illegal and is punishable by law.

ISBN 978-1-4452-3357-4

Dedicated to my lovely wife Helen, my children Bethany & William.

Thanks to Gramps and Nan whose story this is.

Also thanks to all my extended family who appear in parts of this story.

Preface 9

Introduction 11

Growing up in Portsmouth 14

Portsmouth Dockyard 39

Charles Evans 55

Training at Derby 59

Sergeant Major doing a runner 70

Western Desert operations 73

Travel to Africa 76

Battle of El Alamein 78

Arriving at Africa 82

Jeeps name 88

Africa – mine clearance 91

The officer and the mine 96

The Floating Bomb 1942 98

Moascar Stocks 106

Mines 112

Minefields 113

Western Desert 116

Algiers Prison 1942 121

Preparation for Pantelleria 132

Pantallerio 1943 135

Operation Corkscrew 141

Letter received from Home 151

Invasion of Sicily 158

Invasion of Italy 168

Salerno Mutiny – September 1943 175

Italy - The slog northwards 184

Minefield Problems 190

Battle of Sangro 200

Bari 238

Maggie May 243

Cassino 249

Before Anzio 251

Anzio 253

Anzio (Operation Shingle) 256

Anzio Poem 312

Anzio Breakout 315

Rome 325

Audience with the Pope 328

Water point and Rome 334

After Rome 345

Florence 347

After being wounded 364

Tito 375

Stealing meat from the Americans 381

Safe cracking in Italy 383

Last Battle in Italy 387

Middle East 402

The Palestine War 423

Middle East the end 433

7

Returning Home 439

Background Information 442

Life after war.. 458

Speech at his funeral – 13ᵗʰ November 2007 477

Preface

I have put this together from the information that was passed to me by my late grandfather, who I knew as Grampy. Before he passed away he leant me a number of audio tapes which I transcribed and showed him, which he approved. After he died I found a further 12 audio tapes which totalled approximately 16 hours further information on his life and what he did in the war. The Grampy I knew was different to what was in these tapes. In these tapes he reflects back to a time when he was a young man only his 20's, I knew him when he was in his 60's and often would not talk about what he did during the war apart from when he had consumed too many glasses of beer would be when we found out some of what he did.

Grampy was a Portsmouth lad through and through and the stories of his early life are centred on the streets of Portsmouth.

I used the tapes as well as other letters and documents to help increase what the information that I had. I transcribed the tapes and then edited them, putting them into chronological order and making sense of the stories. I have included a chapter at the end of this book with some facts and figures of the family, and the transcriptions of the tapes begin with his own words. I have added any additional comments in Italics to help describe things that were happening at that time.

I have seen this book as the last story that my grandfather, Grampy, told by me as his Grandson.

Introduction

When I do these tapes I am going to give them to one of my grandchildren, so we will see what happens, whichever grandchild, I want grandchildren to do it.

This is all in bits and pieces, so whoever looks at it has to put it together. I don't think that it will be a very good job I suppose. I should imagine that one of my other grandchildren with their computers should be able to put this together. When John's nippers gave me their computer I am afraid it was beyond me, I only hope they will do a better job of it.

I haven't added too many dates of the different battles or when things happened, I haven't remembered all the villages or towns. I have also not told how many dead of OR's means Other Ranks but there are copies there of my units that I was in and the dates I was in, when the commanders would have to make out the details of daily routine. On there you can see the number of deaths of OR's that were missing or where they were. There were two from 626 field squadron and there are two from 23rd Field Company, and there is also a paper on when I was wounded to give some idea. I have got most of the battle companies, and the commanders, you can then work out for yourself the details. I am in one of them. Otherwise I don't know if you can make any head or tails of this, most of these men I knew. There were quite a lot of them. You will only have 4 to look at. You can see by the number of OR's wounded.

Most officers who writes these biographies have maps and dates, I haven't just trying to remember things, as time is going on it is getting harder remembering it all, when different things happened.

Most of the kids think that I don't do much travelling but just have a listen to this. Lahore, Cape Town, Port Tiffic, Bone, Algiers, Augusta, Catania, Calabria, Taranto, Sorrento, Bari, Cairo, Jerusalem, Alexandria, Benghazi, Port Suez, Sudan. Sangro, San Vito, Florence, Venice, Rome, Anzio, Nettuno, Taranto, Deserta, Beirut, Palestine, Greece, Turkey, Egypt, Damascus, the oil pipeline in Persia (which is now Iran), back to Beirut, Damascus, Palestine, Suez, Gibraltar, River Clyde. So you could imagine that is quite a few miles and there are a few more names I can't remember or pronounce.

I had two very good friends in the Army. One was Valentine Middleton, born in Montrose, who died later of cancer in London. He was a union official for the civil service union. The other was James Hardman who died in Bury of a stomach related illness. While they were still living I talked to them by phone or at my house about other members of our 23rd company who also died of cancer.

Growing up in Portsmouth

This is a part of our life as we were when we very very young. Don't forget this was a time when most of the men were unemployed. Most of the boys in our gang were Casey, Doyle, Pink, Gardeners, Knight, the Haydons, the Porters, Fred – my cousin, my brother John and I. Most of us were just helping bringing in the meat, helping our parents. There were also two boys, my mum and my grandparents, as I had no father at the beginning.

Fred O'Neill to the right

I am not saying as a school boy things were better than they are now, I don't think they were as I could remember Father Freely a priest of RC, that used to go to our schools and give breakfasts to some of the children, especially those from Rorke's Drift, and St Johns, and ones that had been moved up in the slum clearing business to Hilsea. The towns then had to transfer to Corpus Christi School.

Fred aged 2 with younger brother John

Grampy at school (2nd row 4th from right)

Uncle George had come out of the army, and he was living with us at our house, as when he went into the service he was living with his mother, which was my grandmother. My grandmother and grandfather were living at that particular time in Wilson Road and we were with them, and they were helping to bring us up as my mother was a widow then.

Before he went into the army he lived with our Gran and Granddad, my mother and of course she wasn't married then. He then went into the Army under a funny position and I will always remember this. Him and a mate called Cochrane, they both came from

Wilson road it was their second offence and they were up front of the beak. The beak was a very notorious magistrate called Ma Kelly. What they did on the second offence was they set fire to a field which was in Army occupation on top of the hill but they were caught and put in the guard room and appeared before the magistrates, and she gave them the option – Army or borstal. Well when he came home and told our grandmother, of course she was ringing her hands out and so was Mrs Cochrane over the road.

    Anyway they decided to go into the Army and this is what happened. Uncle George was an apprentice so he could pick what he wanted to do so he went into the Royal Horse Artillery and after his training he was sent to India. He became light weight boxing champion of all of India. So when he came out he was quite a hero down our street, he was a very good gambler, and a bit of a character. Now young Cochrane with a Scottish name went into the Argyll's.

Uncle George

They done their time and George came out but not Cochrane, he signed on for 9 more years. Uncle George came out quite well up, when the Home Guard was formed he was seconded to it in Portsmouth because they became rocket launching Home Guard. Victoria or Alexandra park not sure which one had this big battery of rocket guns that when the Germans came over, it was terrific noise when it went off. Poor old Cochrane he went and joined his battalion and he was in Hong

Kong and he was taken prisoner. When he came out after the war, his face was terrible. An Australian medic had to operate on him, he had facial injuries from shrapnel and very nearly his entire ear, one of his eyes and all down one side of his face was all puckered up. If he saw when he came out anything Japanese he was well known he went to work on it with a hammer or an axe. If he saw a queue like for fish and chips, he wouldn't stay in the queue he would walk straight to the front and say "I've got this lot for you" no one ever argued with him about it.

He actually came to Leigh Park, of course I am now talking about after I came out of the Army and Uncle George and he used to get nattering together. Two nippers took the Mickey out of his face in Leigh Park. He went after them with a chopper. Before that the Police used to look sideways at him but of course with that they had to do something. For that he got probation but he had to go to the doctors again. The last we saw of him.

Now our gang worked a sort of a co-op and there were about 9 or 10 of us. We grew up very quickly and there were several ways we used to make money to go these pictures which was at the end of our road. We made our money from beachcombing, cockling, whelking and various other means. This was before my mother married and our younger brother Charlie came onto us.

Fred, with brothers John and Charlie

Uncle George would come knocking to do beachcombing and all the coal, coke and bits of wood anything that would burn, he then dumped, and then me and our John would bring it all back. All the stuff we used to bring him for our copper which my Gran and my mother used to go to along with wood and coal. The next thing was the cockles and winkles he used to get, and he used to get buckets of them. We would bring them up in a pram, in a morning before going to school. Gran used to cook them and we used to take them around the neighbours and do quite well out of it.

One day after a storm, Uncle George found what were the remains of a boat and this was our first way of financing as we grew up. I was smashing the boat up, and of course covered in copper plate, which we broke off, and we took it home. The wood we used for the boiler and the copper took to the rag and bone merchant. We did get a large sum of money for this, it was for us anyway.

The second part of how we made money was this; there would be two great big groups along the foreshore we saw Uncle

George out cockling. When the tide was down and there no red flag flying, you could walk down below the water line. We then walked right round as far as we could until we got to Tipner Point, and here was Tipner Rifle range. We would look at the flag and there was no red flag flying and then there would no firing. So the lads would cover us and carry on cockling. We used to have these big straw bags and we would have four or five of them, these we would use for the cockles.

When it was reasonably quiet, two of us would go to the rifle range, we would walk straight through and we were shorter than grown ups. They couldn't see us and the pistol range was at the side. There was thirty yards from the hill which was the entrance. You could see the groups where the target would come up and the bullets would go through the target and hit the bank. This is what we did, we went straight through to the end to the targets, and we put our hands through, you could feel the bullet tops.

We then put them into our bag until we went through all the targets and there was about a dozen. By the time we got to the end it was quite heavy. We would then carry the two bags back to where the groups were working below the waterline, and making sure no one was about of course. When we got down there we emptied all the cockles into one big bag spread the bullet tops into the other bags and put the winkles on top of them. So when the opened up it would just show cockles. We had got enough cockles to sell.

We then go back and by this time the tide was coming in and as we were getting back we would see Uncle George. We could then split up and take some of his and take them back home. We then separated the winkles from the bullet tops.

The cockles that Uncle George got that he sold and we used for some money for the house, but the rest of the winkles we would give out to all the lads and they took them home. What we didn't use we sold. Now when we got enough lead from the bullets we used to take them down the rag and bone merchant. His shop was on the corner facing what eventually became Joan O'Neill's husbands shop, a butcher shop. We used to go in there and for those 8 or 9 ingots he used to give us about 2 shillings or 3 shillings and that went into the kitty to go the pictures for the whole group of us apart from those who had money from their parents.

For the bullet tops, this is where Uncle George came in, he had one of those little pans they used to use join pipes together. We used to put that on the gas stove and we put all the bullet tops on there until they melted. Then we would pour them into a brick. If you know on a brick there is a groove which we would then put the melted bullets into. When we got so much we used to let it cool off and we used sell about 8 of these at a time. The fellow we used to get shot of these with was the rag and bone man. Uncle George would be doing this and Gran would be in the background chirping away "You will set fire to the house you villains".

Uncle George was more or less our father figure as we had no father at this particular time. He was also a very good gambler and he come out of the army which gave him an up beat. He made sure that all our gang of street urcs got money for looking out for things. Like the bottom of Stamshaw foreshore and on the big jetty, gangs used to play pitch and toss. Now we were told to go and watch out for police or suspicious person and then we would run and warn the gang.

We were involved in the greyhound stadium. We used to run the dogs and also clear after the dogs as well after they had done their business. Another thing was cock fighting used to take place on the gas company land. Although we never saw this, we used to be look outs from Victoria and Alexandria park right down to the edge.

Now young Draper the house was the last one which overlooked the ground, so when he opened his bathroom window he could see anyone that was running across the road to warn and all he had to do was put out a coloured mat – red, they would then know on the far side at the gas company grounds where all the activity was taking place.

For all these activities we used to get some money, not much, but enough and that used to go into our co-op fund for when we went to the pictures or when we went to the fair at Portsdown hill. He also gambled on horses and grey hounds and he did very well out of it. We were too young for anything like that. Our Gran who was the sort of the chief of our household didn't go much on him doing things like this. He wasn't married then.

At the beach

By this time of course Mum had married Charlie's dad and Charlie had come into our lives. He was the one who taught us to swim. One day he was home from being on service, and he did do a lot of service, he used to go for two or three years at a time. We were on the Tipner swimming pool which was a place to go, most of us could do doggy paddle. We doggy paddle out to the judges stage and Charlie's dad taught us how to do breast stroke and one that would save a lot of energy. He said it was slower than the dog's paddle all of us were up there. There was one lad who always had trouble with his ear I can't remember his name now, Haley or Ealey or something like that. He had to have a wotsname on and the old man was afraid of putting him in. The old man taught us to dive. We used to go round and round the judge's stage and by the time we had all dived in we could do the actions he was showing. By the time we did this 8 or 9 times we were pretty good breast stroke swimmers. As stepfathers go he was a good decent bloke.

John Britt, Charles Evans sr., and Fred Britt

Now this is what happened when we went to the pictures, this was the Empire Cinema in Stamshaw road. Don't forget now that we had a bit of money saved and I was the Treasurer for the money. The pictures were at the bottom of Wilson Road, opposite the Mother Shipton the pub. The money we were going to use was for the pictures or for when there was a fair on top of the hill, during the holidays. What we used to do was share the money out so we had so much each for rides and various things like that. The money we got to go to the pictures mum gave to me and John. Now we are going on a bit now to when my mother got married and we had young Charlie. These episodes went on through the years until we went to work and started the service or started courting.

Most of the larger lads would go in, but the smaller lads we would save their money. There were three, there was young Charlie now and young Diddy Doyle and young Porter. This is what we did. Three or four of us would go in pay and the rest would hang out side and we would then go into the toilet, and then two more would come in and not be with us. They would go and take the place outside the toilet so no one would come in. Fortunately the lads or men's toilets were on the right side on the outskirts of the cinema. We had two thick and very long ropes which we tied together. At one end we tied to the pipe and the other end we kept on, and this was passed out of the window until it was captured by the lads outside which was a little group including the three little ones.

Charlie was the first one mind you he was a lot lighter then than he was later. Now there three or four of us now that came up one end and they pushed at the bottom until we could pull them in. We carried on until they were all in. The rest who helped the younger ones nipped round the front paid their thrupences and came in. Everybody now left the toilet with our three reprobates and we sat waiting for the film. Another thing happened during the film the person that took the money used to walk up and down squirting, I suppose something to keep the fleas down and this is one of the reasons why it was called the rug hutch or the flea pit.

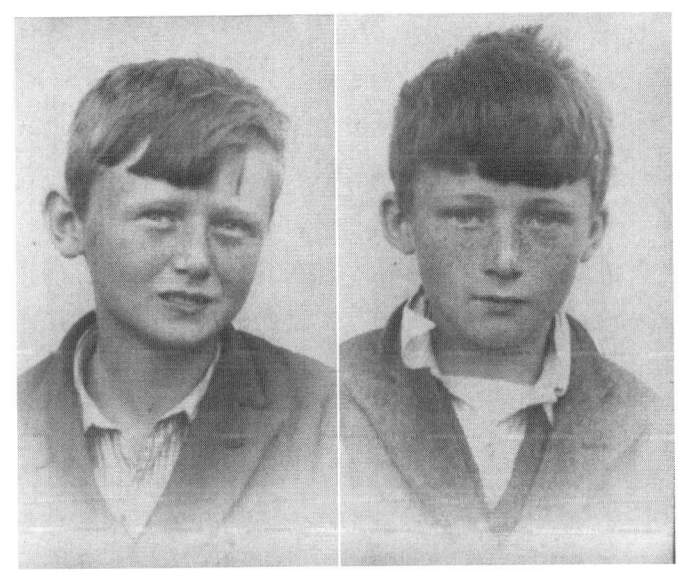

Fred Britt   John Britt

Charles Evans

Now we had an old boat, it was an old boat. It leaked. We kept it at the end of Lower Derby Road where Granny Britt and Ira Britt along with Joan O'Neill would keep an eye on it. The boathouse where we used to bring it up and we would sink it so it was full of water. When we wanted it we emptied and rowed about with it. They would keep their eyes out on it and Granny would screech at anyone who would near it. We used to use it for fishing and various other episodes. We had paddles which Fred kept at his house. Portsmouth was an island and we used it to get around. It had a couple of bridges and we used to lower our mast to go under the bridge into Langs Harbour.

We made a bit of money with the boat, during the hot summers all this mullet and bass came up. At night we had a net which we put across and by the time we hauled them in, especially at the weekends. What we did we would go ashore where the lido was and that was a nice walk. We used then sell them two a penny – fresh fish still alive. We would sell as many as we could. Except the ones we wanted and then off we go. You could only do one of these sweeps a day. I used to go both back home or right round the island, along Eastney, Southsea front, the harbour and back to Stamshaw. Where we tied the boat up and wade ashore. Uncle George would be there and we would see him and we take home any timber home for him, along with cockles. Gran would then clean them.

Fred as a choir boy

There was one little episode which I now consider very dangerous and it was this.

In between Whale Island and Flathouse there were there big panes of timber which belonged to the dockyard. On hot summer days we used to go sunbathing out there and this is how we used to go over there. Four would go in the boat that meant you run under the bridge. Once you went under the bridge it was like shooting the rapids. All the water was running out and so it ran very fast. In fact when Charlie's dad was on sentry and saw what was happening he forbid us to use this boat because I was the one in the boat with our John, Fred, Bill Hatton and Tommy Hatton. That was the four or five that used to use, it was also very low in the water, you had to keep bailing it.

Anyway once you got through the flitting of the rapids, you then went up very casually to the logs and we took the logs over for the day. Soon as the tide started turning, we would go back and we could then walk home along the beach, under the bridge – Whale Island Bridge and out near Lower Derby Road where Fred lived. We anchored the boat or tipped it over so it wouldn't float. When the tide was sufficiently there we would get out onto the stream and then run with the tide and under the bridge back to the boat house. Where we used to keep the boat turn it over and fill it with water.

We used to watch this happen in Wilson Road. You see the vans coming up and the vans were quite rare coming up in those days. They would unload these ponies from the New Forest. It was a large house in Wilson Road and Madgwick was the name of the family. He had quite a lot of garages and stables where they put these ponies in. They always broke these ponies on a Sunday and the man who broke them was a fellow who lived opposite Gran in Lower Derby Road. I worked with him in the Yard when I was a boy. I think he got three pound for every horse he broke. We used to pack the entrance; there was coal merchant's one side and Midways the other side. It was a big square where they broke the horses, they would bring one out and he would do it.

The horses would jump and goodness knows what, they must have been terrified the horses. Everyone was cheering until the horse just stopped and just looked pathetic. He used to ride it up, never had a saddle, he would ride it up Wilson Road and back again.

Then they sold it. Madgwick and the rest of the didicots and they bid for it. The coal merchant next door had two or three and he made sure he had the best when he wanted one. This went on and was part of our ritual, it would happen two or three times a year, but one did stick on my mind.

There was a powerful horse he had and he thought it had been broken and he was going to do the ride of triumph. He got halfway down Wilson road and he took off again, it caught him by surprise and he went up in the air and went straight down on his head with a bonk. I always remembered that our mums house 32 Wilson Road. He always had a gold watch and it came out of his pocket. That hit the ground first and it went all over the road. He had us all out trying to find all the bits and pieces so he could put it together again. I think I saw him with it afterwards so maybe he did put it together again.

We used to go the fair and this happened every year at different holidays by this time we had 8 or 9 shillings and we would share it out. We used to go up with bottles of tea, or water, and cheese sandwiches, and up we would go. We walked up and towards the hill. There we would stay for about 8 or 9 hours. The rides were cheap until we used up our money. We then go home and walk and think about what we were going to do for the following day.

Fred O'Neill and Fred Britt

Portsmouth Dockyard

I was one of the first to go to work, and I was an apprentice on bricklayers - Pitt and Sons – local builders, which I didn't go much on. Unfortunately it was winter and the firm was building the houses at Paulsgrove all I had to do was topping the hearth where the fireplaces where and mix up stuff and do the pointing in the bricks, and it was really cold that winter. I also had to make sure cavity walls were clear. It involved using a bamboo stick and stretching into the cavities.

After 18 months of this our Gran said "I know a better place for you to work" and so she went and saw Mr George Hill who was a chief fellow in the dockyard, he was also a family relative. I used to have to take his two daughters to school. I used to have to go to his house which was in Stubbington Avenue and take them to school. He rather trusted me through all this going across the roads. Anyway he said" One good turn deserves another one" he agreed to take me on when I was 17, but that was 6 months away.

I gave up my apprenticeship and went to work at Streten Brothers And Tanner Ltd, this was a dairy. They were based at Stamshaw Road in Portsmouth. At the dairy were a gang of rather nasty individuals and some of my friend's did not want to work there. I went up to this gang said to them "if you start it I will finish it". Streten Brothers And Tanner Ltd was later merged into Portsmouth Dairies. Another employee at Streten Brothers and Tanner Ltd Dairy was George Voysey, who would later be my father in law.

When my 6 months was up I left there and I knew that I had to report into the dockyard and there I was. I was just a messenger then, but eventually I went onto the cranes and into the workshops, this did me very good, because when I was called up I went into the infantry, and they had so many they didn't know what to do with them all.

Now I shall start at the beginning of my military career. In Portsmouth Dockyard I had to do two nights a week at school, an order came out that if you joined the Territorial's, the Naval Reserve or the Air

Force Reserve we were excused schooling because of the weekly drill. To get permission you had to see the head master of the school. The head master had offices in Portsmouth Dockyard. I saw him and he said "You are doing the silliest thing but I will sign your paper because the country comes first". He signed my paper which I took to my I think it was my inspector. He endorsed it and then I looked around to what territorial unit to join. They were just taking people into a territorial unit but not giving them a permanent unit to drill in.

The one I chose was the 6th Duke of Connaught's Own Battalion, Hampshire Regiment, this was 17th March 1937. The Connaught's Drill Hall was in Stanhope Road, Portsmouth. The main thing we did there was the Coronation of the King George VI and Queen Elizabeth on Wednesday May 12th 1937. Portsmouth Own TA was on that march, it was all the units from Portsmouth TA were there including a few from outside Portsmouth. We also lined the route while he reviewed the fleet, when he came through Portsmouth, this was 20th May 1937.

41

> Gunner '882003'. Frederick Frank George Britt
> Was A Member Of The Detachment
> OF
> "THE 6 BATTALION"
> THE DUKE OF CONNAUGHT'S OWN.
> THE HAMSHIRE REGEMENT. "T A"
> WAS PRESENT AT THE
> *Coronation of Their Majesties*
> *King George VI. and Queen Elizabeth,*
> *Wednesday, May 12th, 1937.*

I can remember when I was a yard boy aged 17 and the Territorial Army was matching though Portsmouth, and that Guildhall was packed. The lord mayor took the salute as he did for the Italian Star association. All those lads served throughout the war when they were called up, the period I am talking about is the period of the coronation of King George VI all the young territorial's when they were eventually called up were sent off to different units. I myself went through Infantry, Artillery, and Engineers before getting demobbed and coming home.

Fred Britt

In July 1938 – As part of the Heavy Hampshire Brigade RA, I went to Plymouth for the weekend as part of TA training. 14,000 men moved into the camp from around the Country. Later in September I took part in King's Cup for Coast defence Gunners for the Territorial Army.

Fred Britt and friend at camp

The Hampshire Heavy Brigade won the Coast Defence Gunners, using their 9.2 in guns. Lieutenant Colonel A.N.R Broomfield commanded the Brigade. The battery number was no. 155 and commanded by Major F.A. Tipple. The battery had the score .470 which was an increase of last years winners at Plymouth. The battery won the Cup and each officer and rank was given a silver medallion by the National Artillery Association. The other batteries were from Suffolk and East Riding Brigades. All three batteries broke the towrope behind the first boat. The wire was 8000 yards away. Hampshire Brigade started first at 12.15pm after poor visibility started the contest. The drill of the men was of a high order. The ramming of the 380lb plugger shell is no light task and the 80lb cordite charges have to be manhandled into the breech before being rammed home.

The medal that Fred Brill was awarded was later taken away to be inscribed with their names and was never given back. It now resides at a museum in Southampton.

The 155th Battery was based at Portsmouth and came under the Hampshire Heavy Regiment, R.A. (T.A.). 28th November

1938 – Converted to Royal Artillery. The 6th Battalion became 59th (6th Duke of Connaught's Own), Anti-Tank Regiment, Royal Artillery. This came under the Hampshire Heavy Brigade.

Then they reorganised the Territorial Army and we found ourselves in the Hampshire Heavy Regiment 155 battery, three batteries from Portsmouth, Gosport and Petersfield. When the call up came lots of the young ones put their ages up so they could join and quite a few did. I remember when I was called up; quite a few were weeded out as they were younger ones. Some of the younger ones from the local TA units were put in at point and a few were killed when they got bombed. By this time a lot of us were abroad but I can remember my cousin who was one of the younger ones saying it was because he was badly shocked by the deaths of some of the young lads that I knew and went to school with. No one has drawn up what did happen to some of our units and where they went and what they did. They had D Day museums, Royal Marine Museums, Royal Navy Museums, but there is nothing about the Territorial Army apart from the Drill Halls.

The call up came for the Munich crisis, and then we found out where our war stations were, part of my battery was on No Man's Land Fort at Spithead. It had 6 inch guns. Our HQ which was at Southsea Castle had 92 guns there and we would have been training on these from when we joined the coastal defence to the present time. We were pretty well equipped we knew exactly what to do with these guns. Whilst stationed here we found food in the basement from World War 1, being nearly 20 years old. As food had started to come into short supply the soldiers stationed there, including me cooked and ate the food! No one died from food poisoning or was ill because of the age of the food.

Fort in Solent in background

Guns operated by Fred Britt – Southsea Common

Fred Britt back row – taken on the fort

49

Later we heard that we were going to stand down but as I was one of the young ones with an engineering background we began an unarmed course which was later to prove very useful. Then went back to the dockyard to carry on working, it was here that I met the girl that I later married Iris Voysey. We met when I used to go down to Cosham and funnily enough she lived in the same street Wilson Road. She was 15 and I was 17. Iris was living at 14 Wilson Road and had been entered into a Lucky Star Photo Competition in the Local paper when I met her.

Fred Britt and Iris Voysey

Iris Voysey

By now all the lads of Wilson Road were joining up, my brother John, Cousin Fred, Ginger Porter, Sawyer, Tommy Doyle, Bill Haughton to name just a few. They all went into the Heavy Regiment. So they started sending different age groups into anti-aircraft and coast defence, anti- tank, as there was obviously a war about to start. Of course everyone was worried about what would happen to us, either killed or wounded. Iris and I did get married eventually before I went abroad.

Now our camp that year was at the Isle of Wight, as they were trying to get us used to where our guns were. There was no battery; there was Spitsand, Horsesand's, No Man's Land and a few other ones on the Island, especially Culver Battery down at Sandown. We had a very enjoyable camp and we came back. Then I and Iris were talking about if war broke out that we would get engaged and I was saving up to have a ring. I think her mother and father were quite alright and there was no argument there. Her father was in the First World War and he was very badly beat up, he was pensioned. His disability pension was 30 per cent. George

Voysey like my dad was a veteran of the First World War. He was part of the 15th Battalion Hampshire Regiment. George Voysey 28936 wounded September 1917 Ypres – Flanders and November 1918 Flanders.

Well we survived for a few months until the actual call up in September for the war. Then things got out of hand and we got our call up papers. We went to the drill hall, and Iris my girlfriend came down there to see us off. Our boat sailed out to No Man's Fort pretty late. So it was pretty late before she got home but she wouldn't leave until we were out of sight.

We then did our time on the fort and eventually they changed us round and we were off to Culver Battery, over on the Isle of Wight. The next thing was they started reading us out again, my army IQ was high, although I couldn't spell, I then found myself in the engineers. When I went there was a corporal and about five of us all from different batteries in Hampshire Heavy Brigade. It appeared they worked on IQ.

Then with four or five of my companions we went on the train to Derby. We went to the Engineering workshops and learnt on fitting and machinists and explosives. I found myself on explosives course. I did a course as an armament fitter I rather liked that job I didn't mind making bangs. When I finished that course I went on a landing craft course, and I was in the 1013 dock operating company. There was also a Sergeant that came down from Scotland. He had a sinister representation. Anyway we all learnt different things about lots of things. On training I first met Denis Healey. He was an officer and he took the high road and I took a lower road to him. The majority of soldiers respected him.

Denis Healey served in World War II, with the Royal Engineers, in North Africa, Sicily and Italy, and was the Military Landing Officer for the British assault brigade at Anzio. Leaving the service with the rank of Major after the war - he declined an offer to remain in the army as a Lieutenant Colonel - Healey joined the Labour Party.

Charles Evans

Shortly after joining the Royal Engineers my stepfather Charles Evans was killed as part of the conflict off Dunkirk. He had served for many years in the Royal Navy and was blown overboard. My mother later received this letter from the Royal Navy. He was a good and kind man.

"Mrs Caroline M Evans

32 Wilson Road

Stamshaw

Portsmouth

Royal Naval Barracks

Portsmouth

4th December 1941

Dear Madam

With reference to the sad death of your husband, Charles A Evans, Acting Leading Seaman, P/J 102286, on war service, I beg to inform you that information has been received from Germany that his body was washed ashore on 12th May 1940, and was buried in a public cemetery, Nordwick, South Holland, and Grave Number 74 S.E. Side.

Please allow me to express again sincere sympathy with you in your sad loss.

Yours sincerely

Commodore"

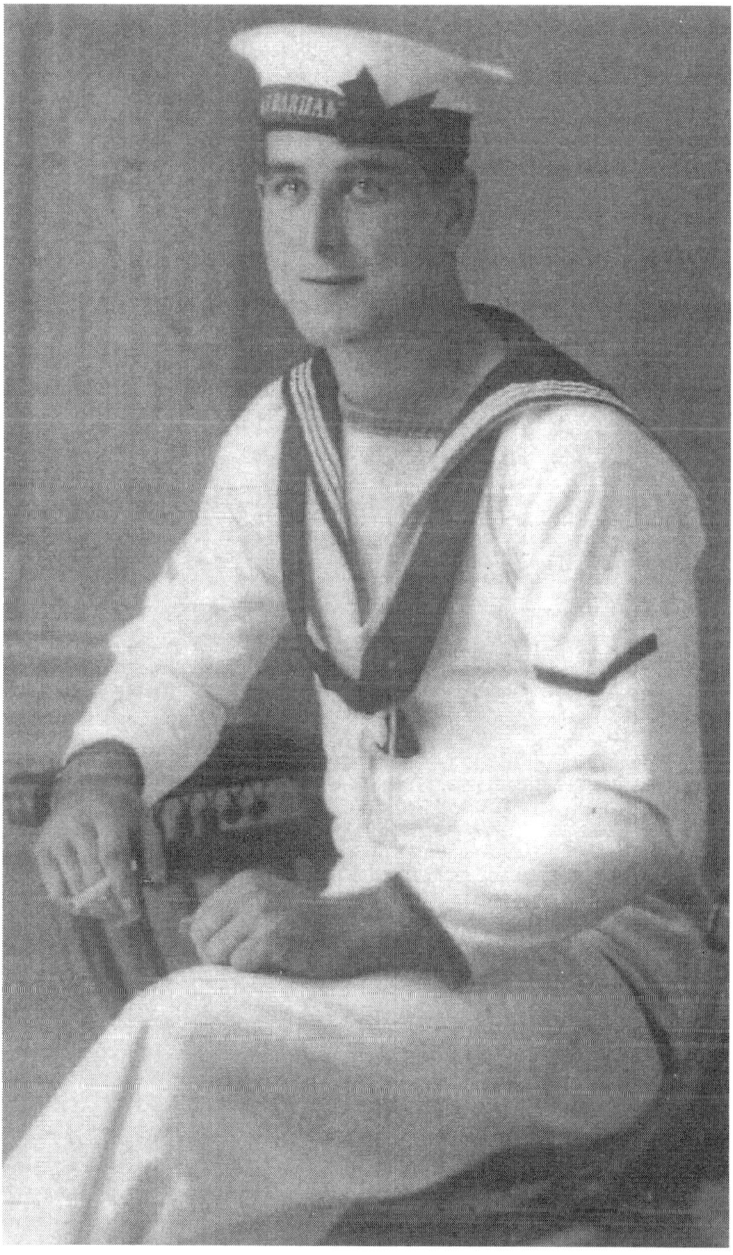

10th May 1940 – Charles Alfred Evans was lost at sea whilst serving on HMS Whitshed. His body was later recovered in the Netherlands where it was later buried. He is buried at NOORDWIJK GENERAL CEMETERY. He had achieved the rank of Leading Seaman in the Royal Navy, and he was aged 38 when he was killed. His service number was P/J102286. On the head stone it states Son of Charles John and Cicely Evans; husband of Mary Caroline Evans, of Stamshaw, Portsmouth.

Training at Derby

There were three sections of us of about 20 men who were undergoing an explosives course. We used to do the course at Donnington as well which was for explosive bombs and mines. We were under tuition of this sergeant Thompson who was an ex-convict and an officer who was an ex-police sergeant, I think, or police superintendent. He taught us about safes and how they used to break into safes they did this on an explosives course. He taught me one of the things to carry explosives was between his legs. He used to use on safes a little breeze gun, I still got one of them that I used in Italy. It did come in very handy once. The police fellow said "that if any of you is caught after this war using some of the things you were taught you will get It very hard." Fortunately I married a very home loving woman and had some smashing children so it never really entered my mind to do anything like that.

Then one night I was just going to sleep when we heard this dull muffled thud and thought no more of it, until next morning when we went off to breakfast. It appeared that somebody with the knowledge of explosives had blown open the safe, which was where the company headquarters was and stolen all of the pay for the whole of the camp. CID came in and they grabbed everybody and we had to make statements.

I will always remember the officer in charge I think he was an ex-RAF but he was too old for flying and he was on administrative duties. He didn't look very worried but he was hopping around there of course the people who were suspected were the ones on the course. It must have been someone in the camp but it definitely wasn't one of ours or our hut because before we went to lights out everybody was in position there were no absentees. To my knowledge until the end of the course no body was apprehended over that little piece.

At Donnington Hall where we did our training it was used in the last war as a German officers POW camp. Behind their fireplace they had constructed a court martial room for anyone who did things they shouldn't have done. I did hear in that some cases they hung officers who they suspected of passing information to the British.

I did a short period with number 6 Commando they wanted an expert on explosives. I went with them to Scarborough and from there we went to the target and then back again. I also saw my first dead German, he was a young German and he died on the way back to Scarborough. He was in full regalia and some of the lads thought he was in the RAF or in the German Equivalent as some of the lads saw wings but then all

Germans had wings including the soldiers. This one was a soldier. When I saw him and I realised there but for the Grace of God go I because any of us could have been killed at any time which I don't think any of us had thought of at that particular time.

The basic training of the sapper was explosives and as I found it very interesting I carried on with it. Most of them went on to putting mines in around the beaches, putting in anti-landing equipment in, mining piers, digging out bombs and blowing up houses during the blitz in various cities. We operated from our main place which was Donnington in Derbyshire. It was an interesting training on explosives. We did some of it with miners, shop firers. They did long drilling holes and put plastic in and then you detonated it.

Donnington was the centre of the bomb disposal, and there is another little story. One of the men that took the bomb out of St Paul's cathedral in London, I think it was Captain Davies. He was an instructor and after the war, he was a very hard drinker he went back to Australia and he was Australian.

He is buried I think in a cemetery in Melbourne.

As I said before they were turning out so many of these dockyard companies and railway companies that the actually wording was quite wrong for what they were doing they were doing various things around Britain like shoring up houses, digging up people in these bombed and Blitzed places.

Our military training was done on the Derby County Football ground, like rifle shooting. As we were trained soldiers we didn't do much of this and went straight into the workshops such as the locomotive sheds where they were building tanks and god knows what else. Eventually when I left we went into Stranra and this was a rest area for the engineers and in-between they had us working on railways and the assembling the docks which was used for D-Day in the landing craft. We used to march down to Stranra football ground for our showers, which was once a week.

I was on HQ and we had two companies over in Northern Ireland and I don't think that anyone would have thought now would have happened then. We used to go across to get bottles of whiskey which was very good or into the Free State for bacon and eggs which we would send home.

When we were on the courses we had a Colonel Hoare who was in charge and when the lads were getting ready to go out on a job he came and gave us a speech. I have never heard a speech like it. It would have done credit to Churchill. In it he said "we can never ever be defeated". It certainly woke the lads up they should have put him on the wireless.

Fred's friends in Royal Engineers

I became the Provo sergeant. How they picked us I don't know, but there was two of us. It wasn't necessary for me to be promoted as I had my money weighed up from the dockyard. So I had to keep off being paid for my stripe. We called to the headquarters and our old man said "Look you two have shown quite a lot of savvy on physical activities like running and football, boxing, wrestling and everything else, would you like to become regimental police?" All we thought we were going to do was guards or fire pickets.

Eventually it came to when we came down to Liverpool. We knew that this would be our embarkation area. In any case it was an adventurous time we were going to take food down to the people down in the docks and unfortunately I ended up running in people who I knew who had pilfered the cargo. One lad who I won't name was a good friend of mine. He was a discipline corporal he was caught he was as a drunk as a hand cart and he had some bottles of whiskey from Scotland on him.

We now found several more and they had found alcohol from some boat or other. The CID was now stopping the convoy of the trucks; there were about five of our trucks or buses. All we could hear was the smashing of bottles of beer that CID were destroying the booze. We then loaded up the British soldiers. My job was to escort them back to our camp and open our cells which had never seen anybody. There was about seven they caught. They were obviously drunk and they couldn't explain what they were up to or where they were. We had to take their boots off and their false teeth out, their braces off and their jack knives off and prepare statements. That was one of the incidents.

One day the officer in charge called all the NCOs' including a sergeant major, and he said to us "I think we have got our marching orders, I will give you something to do in about a fortnights time" As I was doing Provo Sergeant picking up some of the lads but there was a chance now of me getting home – officially. Next minute I knew I had one station which was the house at the Bromborough where we were billeted. I had one and the other one on the other side was my mate Paddy Rooney, he came from Dublin. He was a proper alright bloke.

Cut along story short, the old man called us in "I want this number of men brought back" They weren't absent without leave, they weren't deserters. I got all the ones down south – Portsmouth, Gosport, Petersfield and Paddy got the ones in London and Liverpool.

I was to pick up some men who weren't deserters they had just over stayed leave. Deserters are when they ditch their uniform. These never did and these were caught at the dog track in Portsmouth. They came from Gosport. I went down there when we got permission to do it. Talk about the dirty dozen this was the dirty two hundred. Altogether I think there was thirty that had just come back from being absent and I had to pick up five – three in Portsmouth area which were being held by police and a couple more in London. So I could get down to Portsmouth, then the other escort went and picked up the other ones in Gosport. When I got back to Portsmouth I arranged to meet with Iris and then I got married.

27th September 1941 Frederick Britt married Iris Voysey at Corpus Christi R.C. Church, Gladys Avenue, North End, Portsmouth, Hampshire. He Lived at 32 Wilson Road, Portsmouth. Iris Voysey lived at 14 Wilson Road, Portsmouth. Iris Voysey was a cardboard box maker at a corset factory. The wedding had John, Fred's brother as best man with Doreen (Iris sister) as bridesmaids.

Then we went up to London to pick the other ones up and then caught the train went to Liverpool – Bromborough. They were bringing the other lads in, some from

Scotland, some from Hull and some from Scarbourgh.

So when I got back to Bromborough they were all summarily given so many days detention and put in the guardroom. Unfortunately we only had a small guardroom so we were pretty well wotsnamed. So a lot of them depending on how long they were absent were out in the camp in their own billets. Only two finished in our little guardroom at Bromborough.

Sergeant Major doing a runner

On returning to my unit I met company Sgt major who informed me that the OC was holding an o group for all NCO's regarding movement of the company. We were told all men were to pack all kit and stack it on the parade ground and keep full marching order to ware when we moved off in 16 hours time. We knew where we were going, out to Africa.

While we were supervising the men pack their kitbags on the square the company Sgt major called the junior NCO's together and said "goodbye lads I'm off, i am going on the trot because they are not getting me on a trooper again. I was on the Lancastria when she sank by the Germans on the evacuation from France. So now is the time for you to go if you wish to". Anyway then he said "you are on your last legs now for the UK if you don't take a walk now you'll stay here" and with that he disappeared.

When they were evacuating from France he was on the Lancastria and she got sunk evacuating the troops and there was a terrible loss of life. He was down below and he had to fight his way up, and no body was

70

to get him on a trooper. I could then understand what he said. Later on in my military activity not as bad as that the same thing happened to me. He took a run. Ever since he was frightened of the sea, he said "no body is going to get me on a trooper" and there was a row of troopers on the Mersey waiting for our lads.

In one hour the red-caps were at every gate to stop everyone from leaving, lorries came and took our kit to Liverpool docks and loaded it on to a trooper. The company was then told to fall in and the roll call was made. The officer in charge of the parade asked if the parade was correct and the senior NCO said "one man absent, otherwise all correct" and it was the company Sgt major.

My brother john who i was claiming in to the engineers and our unit, he was on his way and he found himself in Bromborough but we had just left. The men we had arrested were left for him in the hut. This was time later and one of them was the sergeant major and my brother was only a lance jack. He said "how can i be accountable for a senior NCO?" So he said "a lot of funny things happened during the war and this is one of them". He came under the district re, and my lot was on their way to Africa.

Western Desert operations

Tactical overview -On 16 February 1940, the Mobile Division became the 7th Armoured Division. The Desert Rat divisional flash was adopted about the same time. It originated from a sketch of a jerboa drawn by the divisional commander's wife after a visit to the Cairo Zoo.

After the Italian declaration of war, the Western Desert Force was massively outnumbered. However the Italians proved to be no match for the British. The Western Desert Force captured 250,000 Italians in the early engagements in 1940.

On the 13 September 1940 Italian forces from Cyrenaica (now Libya) crossed the Egyptian frontier and advanced 70 miles to Sidi Barrani where they halted to await reinforcements before they resumed their planned advance on Cairo and so began the series of campaigns that marked the three year Western Desert war. For both sides the campaigns were a succession of advances and retreats across open desert and along the coast road. On 5 July 1941 General Sir Claude Auchinleck (1884-1981) took over command of the Middle East. He was himself superseded by General Harold Alexander (1891-1969) in August 1942. In the same month General Montgomery (1887-1976) was appointed commander of the 8th Army, which was formed from the original Western Desert Force.

In the case of the British the campaigns were punctuated by an initial victory over the Italians, then a reversal of fortunes brought by the arrival of the German General Rommel (1891-1944) and the Afrika Korps (March 1941), which continued until the tables were finally turned at El Alamein (October 1942) when Montgomery's 8th Army seriously defeated Rommel's forces. After the victory and hard fighting, the Axis (German and Italian) forces were finally expelled from North Africa in May 1943.

1942 – Fred was sent to Africa and became part of 626 Field Squadron, 4th Armoured Brigade, 7th Armoured Division, and 8th Army. The 7th Armoured Division took part in most of the major battles of the North African Campaign. It also participated *in the destruction of Axis forces in North Africa in Tunisia in 1943.*

Travel to Africa

Off we mustered to our platoon area and our platoon only disappeared on buses through the tunnel and onto the Liverpool docks and then onto the boats. We boarded the Duchess of Richmond and we proceeded up the Clyde well something must have happened my company – C company, was isolated the number that is the number we had for Africa was changed. We got another number painted over our kit bags, which were put up on deck. They went down and we went up. We were walking the deck and this is nasty place. Anyone caught smoking was on a court martial and down in the cells.

It was cold in this evening and we were all laid out on the deck. Down the Clyde we went and an alarm sounded and told to parade at the head of gangway. We were then told to get off by scramble nets and into lighters and they went out into the stream and we went aboard one of the Queens. I am not sure even today which Queen it was. Up we went in and everything was blacked out and into a mess room. We were told not to go out and we had to take off our arms and our boots and put on these shoes and keep our webbing on. We were stuck all along a table.

This explosion happened and I think it was marines, and a hand grenade had gone off in the toilet and there were five or six killed. That was the only thing happened to us. We had hammocks; we slung these, in the morning we had to take them down otherwise you couldn't walk about. In the morning if you walked about you had to put the lifejacket on. I think it was one of the fastest trips they made.

As we were about half way towards Africa we were on our own, there was no body else with us. There were portholes you could look through but they were covered at night time. The crew couldn't tell us where we were going. "Go on tell us where we are?" we said. "Cant tell you" they said. Over the radio came that El Alamein had started and by this time we were now in Cape Town.

Battle of El Alamein

23 October - 4 November 1942

The battle of El Alamein, fought between the British 8th Army (Montgomery) and the Axis forces under Rommel just west of Cairo, resulted in victory for the Allies and was one of the turning points of the war because it marked the beginning of the Allies successful march to final victory. The British, Dominion and Colonial engineers played an important role in that victory. The official Corps history lists the engineering contribution as being:

The thorough preparation of the defences and their completion with tracks, water and other administrative necessities, helped to provide the firm springboard from which the attack was launched.

The efficient and patient clearing of gaps through the huge minefields amidst the stresses and strains of the battle enabled the armoured forces to break through the enemy defences and to rout his forces in the field.

The destruction of disabled enemy tanks and guns prevented their salvage and *repair for further use against the Allied troops.*

All these tasks, and many more, each comprising a number of small operations often carried out by quite small parties of engineers, constituted an important share in the effort of the 8th Army in winning this decisive battle.

During the build up to the final battle of El Alamein (October 1942) the deception plan also required the engineers to build and place dummy lorries on the sites where the tanks and guns would be finally placed. The deception went further with dummy pipelines being laid leading to dummy pumping stations and reservoirs, this work was also conducted in such a way that it led the Axis intelligence to believe that it would be completed long after the actual planned date of the start of the battle (23 October 1942)

We couldn't dock so over the side and into lighters then ashore. We went into a transit camp and from this camp we went first of all going to go to the Red Sea but they changed that, and took us back in land and onto a railway. The railway went right through Africa from Cape Town to Cairo, but part of was under shellfire from the Germans, was derelict. It was called the Cape to Cairo; this is the one that Rhodes built when he was in Africa, a long time before me. German bombs and aircraft had flattened some of the railway.

We got off the ship but by this time things were happening in the top part of Africa, at a place called Alamein. We were on our way to Jo'burg we went up there by train and then we went by plane to Nairobi. From Nairobi we went back on the train and made our way up to a place on the border of Sudan.

There we joined a railway company I knew a lot of people on this company as I trained with a railway company in Derby. We were now not in the Engineers, we were in the Engineers but we were in a re-enforcement company.

Between us and the main body of troops was this thing called Qattara Depression. Our main job was to load water into jerry cans, we had those big square petrol cans which were rubbish, you only had to tap them and they burst. We tipped the petrol or diesel into these jerry cans which were either captured or we had made by the Egyptians by some of the factories there. These jerry cans were then ferried across in Lysander's and Hanson's and old aircraft and into the desert for the troops to get hold of.

A funny thing about all this manoeuvring around when we were in the UK getting ready to over to Africa we got kitted up with pith helmets. As soon as we landed we went to the nearest dump and made a big dump of them, never saw them again. The only time I saw them was on the South African troops. It wasn't until the Japan one fell over we went to show them the flag in Persia and Syria that we wore snake hats. As soon as we got back to Egypt we ditched them and put on berets.

Arriving at Africa

When I came into the 8th Army, we were supplying the army by air with petrol, water and diesel. We used it before and after the battle in Libya. When the battle was over the Go Boys which was an army division had been decimated and so there was a big re-enforcement unit from the remnants of other units. We joined this and we joined the 626 field squadron. This was part of the 7th Armoured Division and part of the 4th Armoured Brigade. We went straight to nearly the end of the war. I think it was the Go Boys they had traffic lights as their division sign.

We used to go in these Lysander's and we used to drop off this stuff at different places, and the Sanuss, the Arabs, they hated the Italians, they were alright with the Germans and the British, but they were the ones we had to carry gold sovereigns for. We carried five each in case we crashed and they would take us back, but we had to give them these sovereigns. The railway we saw damaged. We could see what they were doing; these railway companies were putting the lines in and all that. They were now joined by a Madagascar or some where like that, and they were going like the clappers. According to the wotsname it went from the Red sea to the big depot they were building now at El Alamein. We now went in and there was a hiccup. Our company more or less intact but job now was finished and it only went on for a couple of weeks.

After this they were progressing well with this railway every day we went to see how far they had gone, and of course the aircraft from the Luftwaffe or from the Afrika Corps did now not trouble them. Eventually they did get as far as Cairo. This line was called Cape to Cairo, and it was made by Sir Cecil Rhodes, it came in very handy by now, but of course now supplies were coming up this line and going into Cairo by this time the Royal Navy had supremacy in the Med and our Air Force was not even challenged. Occasionally we saw luftwafte and by this time we were now in a re-enforcement unit with the RE's, we went and joined a squadron, which hardly existed, and it was a division, which had really been knocked about called the Go Boys. On their sign were amber, green and red, like on a traffic lights and that was their divisional sign. They called them the Go boys, and they did Go too I don't know where they though! They were two brigades down and they were putting everyone in to make this brigade up.

We then dropped them for our Long Range Desert Group and another force we called Popski's Private army. I never knew this though until some time in Italy, when Popski's private army was the reconnaissance of the 8th Army. It was no. 1 demolition group was its proper name; the long range desert group was the long range desert group. These two were very part of the ancestry of the 8th Army

Popski did die but he died in London. His ancestry was a bit of a puzzle, Popski that wasn't his real name was a product of Egyptian, British, Russian, Belgian, take your pick.

Popski's Private Army was an effective, albeit irregular, unit of British Special Forces founded in Cairo in 1942 by Major (later Lieutenant-Colonel) Vladimir Peniakoff DSO MC (1897-1951). PPA was one of several irregular units spawned in the Western Desert during World War II.

Peniakoff was nicknamed "Popski" by the Long Range Desert Group's Intelligence Officer Bill Kennedy Shaw because the signallers had trouble with his surname. Peniakoff had some unconventional ideas about discipline and techniques. Indeed there was little conventional about Popski or his men - Popski himself was not a Briton, but a Belgian (of Russian parentage). Brigadier "Shan" Hackett grumbled that Popski expected to be paid for running his "private army", and that complaint was the origin of the name. Nonetheless, the unit was officially formed as No 1 Demolition Squadron, PPA, and part of the 8th Army, to attack Rommel's fuel supplies at the time of the Battles of El Alamein.

Specialising in behind the lines raids, PPA caused problems to the enemy for a short while in North Africa and then mainly in Italy. They entered Italy at Taranto as part of the advance guard of the amphibious landings. By the end of WWII, PPA had destroyed several Axis aircraft and thousands of gallons of fuel, and had taken roughly 600 Italian prisoners. The value of their *reconnaissance work is hard to assess, but considerable.*

626 field squadron

A few days after again we were changed we became 626-field squadron, no, 6-field squadron the 626 came later. We joined the 7th Armoured Division but we were in the 4th Armoured Brigade, which was separate. Now this time we went up as far the Germans were making the last ditch-stand, when this was over come we found our way up and over to Cape Bon where the Germans had now all gone in. In the distance I did see one of our battleships, which was bombarding Bone. Eventually they sent one of our Indian divisions to mop up, now there was two little episodes that happened apart from the give and take of mine warfare, taking mines out, we never put mines in and getting our armour moving was our main objective.

I already had met Valentine Middleton and others by this point and by this time another lad had joined us. He was a refugee from a Lancashire regiment and he was getting on in age, his name was Jimmy Hardman. Jim, Valentine, "Tosher" Stokes, and another one that came from our squadron were in our section.

Jeeps name

Another thing I would tell you were my mate's change of names that was Valentine Middleton, his mother must have picked that name because if she picked he deserved to have it called and that was his name. He didn't go much on it and then it changed like this. His brother was in the Highland Division I think he was on the Argyll's. Then one night on stag he was talking to me and he said "I would like to see my brother I saw him in Alec but I haven't seen him since". I said " Do you know where they are?" and he said "Yeah" You know we call them the island decorators, he says "there trail is well blazed", and it was right through the desert. Their HD's was up all over the place, they were a very proud division.

Suddenly there was a jeep and the old man came up and he nodded to us and said "What you doing stag?" and we said "yeah" because there was little discipline apart from when we were bullshitting. We carried on walking round and then he went to the mess. Val Middleton walked across to the jeep, and the keys were in it. "Right" he said "here is my rifle take it back" he says "I am off do a bit of cover" and he disappeared. When our stag was up I knocked up the other two that was going to relieve us, and we would pass it on from one to another. The only thing we were worried about in the desert was getting run over. We got our heads down and two days later, and the old man went spare when he found out his jeep was gone. That word has a big significance.

    Two days later in rolled Jeep as he was now going to be called. He had three cracked ribs, two beautiful black eyes and what had happened. In some of the roads in the desert they put roundabouts to slow up traffic. They put these big tins of oil – empty and now full of sand around in a circle, of course Jeep being half a sleep tries to get through one. The four wheels of the jeep just come off; of course Jeep went for a walk. He did find his brother, he saw him and his brother patched him up and got him a lift right to our camp with one of wagons that were going down there. He came on parade that morning, and from that morning that was when his name changed from Val Middleton to Jeep Middleton.

Our sergeant and he was a good one he was, he was at the back and we were all getting examined. Jeep could just about stand up and all of a sudden we heard a voice going "Jeep, Jeep, Jeep" of course everyone looked at poor old Jeep as everyone knew he had taken the old man's jeep. From that day on I never heard any other name but Jeep for Middleton.

Africa – mine clearance

We were clearing mines in and between Benghazi and Tobruk. The 1st Infantry Division were getting ready to have a go. One day after clearing the mines we were talking about different aspects of the war. A Zanussia came in – now the Zanussi were scouts for the Arabs, and were very opposed by Mussolini. He said there were mine fields further out. Our section was detailed and off we went with him. About 30 of us went out in these big Whites cars – big army cars. He led us out and eventually came to the debris of some army jeeps and weapon pits. They were men of the rifle brigade and they had been over run by the Germans, they were really done in. There were a number of dead in the slit trenches and they were lined up like in the Wild West films. The armoured cars were in a circle and the men had tried to dig in, and get some cover. They must have surprised by a German armoured division.

Some of the weapons pits were filled with sand and the remnants of the men were lying around. It was first time I knew that men's finger nails and hair grew when they were dead. There was one grave – it was a weapon pit that had been turned into a grave, and there was a colonel in there which reminded me of the lieutenant- colonel they tried to kill or capture Rommel. He had his first aid dressing in his hand and he was holding it towards his stomach. As thought he was trying to cover something, a wound or something. In the bottom of this weapon pit was a prayer book – you couldn't tell their age or what time they were over run – what year as this was the last final run through Africa.

The mine field was merely Hawkins grenades. These were wired and some could be seen. Once we got through and lifted the minefield, one good thing was that they were all tied together with a piece of string like sausages and unfortunately the German armour had blown them apart.

A grave recognition unit was then sent for and they came up and took what was left of the men away. That was an important part. We took them back for I would imagine a military funeral. There was no smell, only a couple of birds flying around. There could have been the best part of a company of men. The Colonel that was there was the son of an Admiral that was one of the horrible parts of the war. It wasn't really the war it was the left over's of the war. The Admirals name was Keyes, the son of course was Colonel Keyes, and I think he was given the Victoria Cross.

This happened in Africa, this is one of the final pushes. The time we went past Benghazi.

Egypt

Another incident that happened that was quite interesting. While we were waiting one of the officers he was the commander of Popski's Private Army he had a Russian sounding name but he was British. He took us to see one of the wonders of the world, during the bombing all the artefacts from Tutankhamen were stored in a safe place in the Valley of the Kings from the museum where it was in Cairo, Egypt. We had a very good verbatim on everything that had happened up to then. Later it did come to Britain after the war of course. It went on show in the London Museums. I carved my of an Admiral that was one of the horrible parts of the war. It wasn't really the war it was the left over's of the war. The Admirals name was Keyes, the son of course was Colonel Keyes, and I think he was given the Victoria Cross.

This happened in Africa, this is one of the final pushes. The time we went past Benghazi.

Egypt

Another incident that happened that was quite interesting. While we were waiting one of the officers he was the commander of Popski's Private Army he had a Russian sounding name but he was British. He took us to see one of the wonders of the world, during the bombing all the artefacts from Tutankhamen were stored in a safe place in the Valley of the Kings from the museum where it was in Cairo, Egypt. We had a very good verbatim on everything that had happened up to then. Later it did come to Britain after the war of course. It went on show in the London Museums. I carved my name into the Great Pyramid at this time – "Fred was 'ere!". Just like to leave my mark behind.

The officer and the mine

I was a minder with two other sappers on one of our officers. We were reccing a lateral road on minefields. Mines had been reported, and unfortunately we did find one. The officer trod on one or set off something, I don't think it was a big mine but it was enough to blow him to bits. Unfortunately I caught a bit of the blast and also a bit of his blood. My bush shirt and shorts were saturated with it. In fact we had mines on us but they were disarmed. They were hanging on us. When the stretcher bearer came up I could walk but our officer was dead. When I got to the regimental outpost most of the blood had dried. I had a small cut in my leg in my shin. When the doctor got my vest, shirt and shorts off he couldn't find anything. So he said "take him out and give him a scrub down" The time they got all the blood off me I had nothing wrong with me.

So I got my shirt and pants and went back to my unit. I got a new shirt, a new singlet, new trousers and a new pair of boots. Unfortunately I had to make a report about the mines we had to found so when our bulldozers came along it was comparatively safe. The mines were pretty regular for anti-tank and in half hour they had cleared this road ready of course for the battle.

The Floating Bomb 1942

We were then paraded and about 24 sappers were picked to do a job and flown into Henderson field, which we know now was in Jordan. I was still a corporal and there were four corporals and all of our members were from the beach group.

Henderson Field was a rough landing ground; most of the planes seemed to be Rhodesian or South African. It was an RAF staging area. There was a quite a lot of, Dakotas, and Lysanders planes. It was an airport at the front, with planes going in and out, there were damaged planes landing all the time.

We stayed at the Field and then we got buried down for the night. We were told the job wasn't for anything important and so after getting acclimatised the following morning there was a plane, which flew us across, which we know now, across the canal, further up, I should imagine it was the Red-Sea.

When we landed we were taken into lorries and we were taken to the point where we were supposed to work. We found there was a steamer, a very old steamer, but she was off shore. When we got there we had to report to the crew of the ship. The crew of the ship was Greek. They were already ashore in a camp, the ship was dead; when we got there we made ourselves known.

The captain said, "There is so much petrol loose in there, that boat is a floating bomb". He said, "that it was full of petrol" and they were frightened the Germans will fly over and bang it one, but what had happened a bomb had dropped on it but it had gone right through it and out the bottom. Of course the crew went to crash stations and patched up the hole whilst the water was kept out. As soon as you got near it you could smell the petrol. So the ship, besides being half full of water, was also half full of petrol. That was one of the reasons they had shut down anyway we carried on now discharging the ship. It was a danger just to be there especially if we were attacked by the luftwafte or anyone smoked. You could see the fumes coming out of the hatches.

There was a pioneer section from Mauritius they had built a jetty, floating pontoons out to the ship and they were like big lighters which we found out she was packed out with flimsies – petrol. These flimsies, you only had to look them at them and they broke, they were made out of a square tin not like the old Jerry cans that we had. We used to call them some inferior name, not as well as the German jerry cans. We got them out in these flimsies. We transferred it into Jerry cans; most of these jerry cans were actually captured. There were some that were getting made now by the Egyptians.

When we got there we got aboard, there were four corporals, and I was still a corporal. We each took one with our section into a hatchway. There were four hatchways. There was no winches working, most of the winches that were working, were constructed by block and tackle. The Mauritian company had rigged up the derricks, all the derricks were up, what they used to do, by hand, the thing down to put the flimsies on lift it up, pull it ashore, or pull it over the gunnels, and down onto these big rafts. When they were filled, the rafts that is, they were pulled ashore, or rowed ashore and then transferred into lorries.

If they leaked we poured them into jerry cans and they went off somewhere high, I haven't a clue where they went. All I remember is the divisional sign of the lorries was a camel, which was appropriate. As soon as we got enough the lorries come up and took the jerry cans away. If the flimsies never leaked they put them on wagons and they went off. The ones that were filled went off to somewhere else. Most of the flimsies I think went to an airfield where it was dropped to the long-range desert group or Popski's private army. These were units operating behind the troops at El Alamein. You could hear the noise the bangs that they made by couldn't see anything.

There was a continuous evaporation of petrol from the hatches, especially in the heat. We had to rig up big canvas shutters, which carried air down into the hatches; there were four of them. We had to close up at night time, in case there was a sand storm. You only worked done there for so many, well half an hour at a time but if there was a wind especially in the evening, it did clear some of the smell away.

We got down about half way through the ship. A much contracted four days, and it was exhausting work, especially for the black lads, who were from Mauritius had to pull these big like number of flimsies and get them ashore and onto these big raft things. By this time we could get torches and have a look at what this bomb that had gone through. It had gone right through and gone out through the bottom. It had just missed the shaft that drives the ship, the long shaft that goes right through the ship. They had put timber, bedding and god knows what to block this hole. The bilges were quite full of petrol, because they had a rough so and so.

As we got further down the ship we could then get in pumps and put it into big canvas tanks, which we had ashore. It went off to one of these transit camps where they got the petrol out of the salt water. Petrol was in short supply.

Anyway we knew there was a bomb that had gone right through but what we didn't know there was another bomb until about half way down. The next thing was we stopped for a bit as one of the men had found a set of fins. This has gone through and ended up on the floor of the crew's quarters and we had to then think how to get it out. We couldn't disarm the thing, first of all we didn't know what tools to have but it wasn't ticking, we assumed at the time it was overcharged.

The problem now was how to get this thing out. It was still leaking petrol from flimsies in the ship. We stopped all work, we managed to get a line round it and we pulled it out with muscle by using one of the derricks. We were going to get it out and sling it over the side. Then one of our officers came up and said "No we had better not do that" he says "we will get some explosive and a fuse and we will lower it over the side a bit further out".

We then rigged up the tackles that were lifting the flimsies out and managed eventually to pull the bomb up and onto the deck. We then put the charge over the filler cap on the bomb and with a detonator on it lifted it up with a derrick as now we could lift over the side. We put it on a raft, rowed it out until we got about 200 yards from the boat. We went out into the red sea; we were on the extreme mouth of the canal. We activated the fuse, lowered it over the side, rowed like hell back to ship, and then it fired. A great column of water went up in the air, hundreds of fish came up and the Mauritian's rode out and they got buckets full and so did the crew. We had those fish. The cookhouse was ashore and this Greek wotsname cooked all the fish. They cooked them in these big camps they had. Anyway we had a nice supper anyway.

We started to get right down to the bottom of the boat; we got all the petrol out. We then had to get a pump, and pump the bilge water out to the beach, it went into tanks as half it was petrol, these flimsies you only had to look at them and they burst. Anyway quite a lot of them, these coloured lads were transferring them into jerry cans that they had captured or we had captured. I suppose that petrol was quite all right and taken up the canal and dished out the armies – 8th army.

When the ship was more or less dry, we then went down and found where the hole was, where the first bomb had gone through, and they packed bedding and there was a covering of wood over the top as it wasn't leaking all that much. We left it by now the captain had decided it was a bit safer and they got up steam and they eventually went to some shipyard to or beach to get this hole covered up with steel.

We then went ashore where we got our marching orders. Instead of going back to Henderson field or to our other beach group we now found ourselves on our way to reinforce the army. There were some terrible shortages, the shortage of troops. Rather than go back to Henderson field we went to a transit camp just near the great lakes.

Moascar Stocks

Now we found out where we were, we had heard nothing from our beach group; they had gone right across the other side of the Mediterranean. Eventually the people in command said "you are bloody sappers" join up with this one. When we saw this wotsname he said, "right do you know much about mines?" well we knew something about teller mines, he said, "right you go to Moascar, and that was the engineer place on the canal, and we learned something called Moascar stocks. The Army had an establishment called the 'Middle East School of Military Engineering', which was based at Moascar in the Canal Zone of Egypt.

In the first campaign the advancing British troops met considerable numbers of mines in the Italian defensive positions. These were detected and located by the observation of disturbed soil and probing with bayonets. After the Afrika Korps arrived (March 1941) and with them the reversal of British arms in the Western Desert, the British began to use mines to cover their withdrawals. Their mine stocks were extremely low so the Royal Engineers used recovered Italian and German mines, as well as, mines built in hastily established factories in Egypt.

The experiences of both laying and clearing mines during the early stages of the campaign taught the engineers valuable lessons. Early in 1942 a Royal Engineers School of Mine Warfare (Major P Moore, Royal Engineers), was established near El Alamein. Its objectives were:

- *To find out the best way to breach or make gaps in minefields.*
- *To evolve and teach standard drills for clearing mines and recording the laying of minefields.*
- *To try out ideas, devices and expedients this might be proposed.*

We now heard about the school of engineering and although most of us had done mine work and explosive work and the occasional bomb; they said, "You have to go through the course again". This was where we came into contact with the Moascar stocks. The instructor was an Australian. I don't know if anyone has heard of Moascar

Stocks and it was very ingenious. There was a door with two armholes, which you put your arms through, in front was a big box full of sand and they put a mine in. Of course you couldn't see it only feel it, which is the way they taught you. The instructor use to make us identify it and disarm it, find the booby trap and move onto the next one. You would go through at least 7, 8 or 9 and after that he was considered an expert on mines. This was to make us use to mines.

We done three types of teller, (which was a round metal mine, a German Anti-personnel Mines) and two types of S mine (Schrapnellmine). With the S-mine, you could only see the four spikes sticking out of the ground. The mine would burst at your feet, come up to waist height and burst again. We would probably do more mine work than any of them there. In the UK we put mines down on the east coast, around Hull and that way. Again as they always say about offices and gentlemen, it was the O R's that armed them and took back the pins to make sure they were there ready to detonate. We never put in never put mines in again in my war service, two parts, one when we left

Italy to come in back to the Middle East where we are now and the other one was in Anzio that was the only two places we put mines in apart from the UK.

We were down in Moascar and we were learning about these new floating baileys. In the background was a memorial to the Australians that fell in the First World War at Gallipoli and in the desert. I knew when my father come home they were in a terrible state but the last final fight that they had. I thought my father in the Hampshire regiment along with the Australians and New Zealanders were survivors of various battalions. This was their last battle before they evacuated Gallipoli; they tried to take some sort of position. Wars were a bloody mistake. Gallipoli was a terrible mistake and something similar happened to me of course when I was in Anzio and the funny thing was the man that had something to do with both of those was the Prime Minister – Mr Winston Churchill.

They were beaten about, my father when he came home, of course. When he died I was only two and my brother John was only one. He said how terrible it was there, the man who sent him there. Well he was in hospital when he went back to Africa before he went into France and there was an Australian with him. In fact my aunt very nearly married him. Unfortunately when they got better both of them went to France and the Australian was killed. In 1916, my father Corporal Frederick Waldemar Britt was discharged from the army but all his papers were missing the place they had been stored in was hit in the Second World War and asbestos was among the papers.

One other little thing, this happened in the desert. We often wondered from our point of view, the Australians if they captured a tank they used to paint a great big kangaroo on it not the British flash, so it was bit funny to see (and it was easily painted too), the Italians or Germans could paint it. We were told to handover to the Australians or any repairs of a certain tank that the Italians had. We found out afterwards, or I did, that the engine was a British engine but under contract and copyright to the Italians and so any engines or tanks we captured the Australians could do anything to them and they all talk about lateral discipline. They seemed to be a much disciplined lot from what we saw of them and very smart too. If they ever become a republic I will miss that bloody hat.

Mines

Before 1941 mines played only a small role on the battlefield, but in the Western Desert massed armoured formations and largely featureless terrain combined to create ideal conditions for the use of mines in a defensive role. Across the coastal strip there were few features that could be used for defence, so mines, along with barbed wire, offered the only economic means of defence.

To clear a minefield the Engineer originally had nothing more than the tip of bayonet to feel for mines with, but during the war in the Western Desert a "Mine Detector" became available. This used a sensor, which detected the variations in the earth's magnetic field caused by the metal in the mine. This did not always work, which meant the bayonet had to be used again, but as the war progressed they became more reliable.

Minefields

Now this is how you put a minefield in. You couldn't recognise minefields, you had to crawl forward, put a mine down, cover it up and get back again, if you were still alive. To do it probably you found a datum, you had a compass bearing and a map reference. You then went straight ahead from the datum to where you wanted the end of your minefield to be. Then there was the tape man; he took his tape out to the datum. When the man came along the datum and dug the holes in, say two feet apart, two feet apart, until you got ten mines in.

Now the armourer came out, he put the detonator in after removing the pin, and so on until his ten mines were now armed. He then went to the end mine as far as we could go; we would just keep it in an ordinary triangle. Every two or three you put in a mine, the armourer would come along, put in a detonator, pull out the mine, and then you would put in another mine and so on. Until the line along the front and that would be the German side would now be armed. You now have got those ten pins, the armourer has, the OR. Not NCO; never found an NCO who

113

put a mine in. Never seen an officer put a mine in, Only OR's. Now the armourer was an OR, OR means other Ranks. A term I distinctly disliked. As I said before our mothers gave us a name when we were born and the Army made it, as we didn't exist.

So we got ten pins from there and the ten pins from there. We would keep it nice and square, ten there and ten down there. So then they got 10, 20, 30, 40, 50, 60 pins. You then met up with your party, you withdrew the white tapes, and you then had all the pins in your hot hand. You went up, now the officer he was making a map. He would then let you hand over to the senior NCO or the officer that was making the map. Now the pins were passed to the officer that made the map, now I don't know where it went from there. There were so many pins of those detonators that these number of mines. You then got your shot of rum and went off to beddy byes. Now, that is how you done a correct minefield.

We were clearing minefields to get some of our men out that were killed and to get into some of their mine fields they vented a cordex net. A cordex net was fired over and went over the mine field, and then you exploded the net, as this was explosive and it detonated the mines. That was the theory. We used to fire it from small mortars one each side but unfortunately it jerked up in the air and it enclosed one of our mates. Of course when it fired it killed him. After that we relied on our bayonets to find the mines as I say with all the heat and flies and god know what else.

The drills taught at the School proved their worth. In preparation for the battle of El Alamein (October 1942) the engineers used the drills to lay minefields and during the opening phases of the battle (Operation Lightfoot) they used them to successfully clear routes through the Axis minefields, the 'Devil's garden', of about 500,000 mines laid in two major fields running north-south across the whole front with a total depth of about 5 miles, to allow infantry and armour formations to move forward and engage the enemy.

Western Desert

Divisional engineers activities

Throughout the Western Desert campaigns the divisional engineers were engaged in their usual role of providing bridging, constructing defences and removing obstacles, but the peculiar conditions of the desert meant that a lot of their energies and resources were taken up providing a water supply, deception (camouflage), airfields, and mine defences and clearance.

Water

One of the primary tasks of the engineers throughout the Western Desert campaigns, fought in very arid conditions, was to provide a water supply. This entailed locating water on selected routes, boring for water, cleansing water, installing water pumps, water storage facilities and laying water pipes. During the periods of retreat the engineers were responsible for denying water to the enemy, this involved dismantling or destroying water facilities and pouring 'bone oil' into water wells.

Deception (camouflage)

The vast open spaces of the desert made it difficult to conceal forces and their activities; to over come this difficulty the engineers were employed in creating appropriate deceptions.

We had had a few little Barneys as this was done by our tanks and we were miles away. We used to use scorpions just to belt our way through. Of course there was no mines now the Germans and Italians were packing it in as fast as they could until we got to Mareth. Now another army had come out I think it was an airborne army. After a few days they had retreated into Cape Bonne, and here they surrendered. There is a bit in here about the surrender.

We now had the Germans on the run. We had chased them from Tripoli to the beginning of Cape Bonne. The whole of the Allied Army was more or less in a half circle around so that they had the sea behind them. There was quite a lot of shellfire coming and going, in Cape Bonne on the remnants that were hiding in there. We moved up more or less by accident we were there at this point, as we were trying to put a wide track through a mine field. There was tracks made through but we were widening them, and we were under shell fire. Our squadron was widening about three tracks. We had to go through our covering people who were the Queens Regiment – light infantry. There was now a half circle of the 1st Army, the Americans, the French and the British 8th Army. Sappers of all the lot were working on these mine fields. When suddenly there was a quiet that come down. Just the occasional explosions that came from Cape Bonne, and we had naval ships of the coast as well. Where they were firing I don't know.

Then there was a lot of parlaying and telephoning, but when the Germans pulled through their own minefields as a rule, they upended everything. So normally there was a recognition that you were on a minefield either from our side or from their side. Of course when they were retreating they took most of it out, so we were on bayonets, trying to find the mines. We did find a few of what we called jumping jacks. That's the mine that jumped up in the air – terrible things, but very easy to disarm if you found them.

We had gone right through to the end of the mine fields when we heard; they were talking about packing in. We heard the New Zealand General – Field Marshall was going to take the surrender along with another General. Rommel wasn't in this capture but the rest were. The RAF was climbing on top of them, the Navy was at the back of them and the Army was in front of them, oh and the Indians were there as well. Eventually we went in and after a time out came these two German generals with the surrender and they signed the documents of surrender.

Now we were told to go back as far as we could. Make sure the mine fields were clear and mark them. Then the Germans and Italians surrendered and there was quite a big march. We had to clear a large area for them to go through. One side they had put their equipment and the other side they had to drop their arms. Then they had to go into this area where all the red caps from the different units, and we had to get out of the way. We went a bit further into North Africa.

The end of the axis in Africa I can tell you a few of some of the things that were affecting me in the service. First of all I

119

think was watching the end of the British Raj, Australians, New Zealanders, Canadians, it was everybody who was anybody in Africa. The Australians were going home to fight in the islands and we were going on to Italy. We were going to miss this but the New Zealanders came with us and came over to Italy as well whilst we were getting ready for this we had a few funny episodes.

Algiers Prison 1942

We went to Algiers, where we met French schoolteacher and his wife, Augusta and Bertha Villan.

Bertha and Augusta

There was a lot of French that would take you in and give you your tea, and this couple, me and Jimmy Hardman, and they were with the Free French. They befriended us and they showed us the wireless set, a square one, which they used to use to transmit their signals to Gibraltar, regarding anything that had happened in Algiers or

North Africa. They operated from where they lived, they operated from a huge block of flats, and you couldn't miss it, as soon as you walked into Algiers you could see it. From their vantage point, as they were right at the top, they showed us the masts sticking out of water of all the ships that had been sunk from when the 1st American Army came ashore.

If you were a religious person but the first time we were in Algiers, we were walking with our friends Augsusta Villan and his wife, Bertha. They wanted to go to the cathedral in Algiers for high mass to celebrate the Bastille. Anyway we went, this was the first time we had been in a church in Africa or French church in Africa. It was more ceremonial than being in British churches.

After we cleared the Germans from Tunis, the last city that we entered, there was no fighting. The Germans were then held up in Cape Bonne, but they had no Dunkirk. Out in the sea was the Navy they made sure that they didn't get off. We then sent our Ghurkhas in to get the surrender of the Germans. We then were taking them back to the ships that took them to America.

The Defeat of the Germans at Cape Bonne, most of the units were brought in to take prisoners down to Algiers. We used to pick the train up at Béjaïa after the Germans have marched from Cape Bonne and we ferried them down to the ships at Algiers that was taking them to America. We done two or three trips first and the final trip, was a very good one. Then they got us organised and the trains came up and the prisoners had to go Algiers. The first train came, and we took them down to Algiers just outside called MasonCary. All the way down there the French were shouting and screaming. We were now on our way to Tunisia, we were transporting prisoners and we were in a big long train. We were in the cattle truck. Every time we stopped the locals would run out and give us wine.

We picked up the Germans at Setief and we took them on to Algiers. We used to have a special drill as some of the Germans used to burn there way through the carriages. So at the end of the train we used to have an iron bar with iron chains just touching the ground. So if anyone got through he had a bit of a job to get through the end of the train.

The next trip back, there was a train ready for us, going the same way more or less. We went into our unit; of course they were coming down like no ones business – the prisoners I am talking about. They loaded them up and off they went. On the third trip was the most ambitious as we ended up in prison in Algiers.

There was a man in Algiers who ran a restaurant, he was English, and he married an Arab girl, and he was ex-foreign legion. Some of the boys used to bring down their souvenirs and sold them to him, including money, but this last was a bit of stormer. We had filled our water bottles unfortunately with vino which was pretty cheap and on the way down; when we had our break we used to drink the vino and two lads from Liverpool who had mixed dealings with this sergeant.

The sergeant in charge of our section was the most hated man that God had put on this earth. He was a Geordie, he had an MM from the 1st world war and he was just about on this last legs. The company sergeant major was the one who unfortunately, got what was left of our beach group and made them put their tents up, very pukka, long lines very handy for the luftwafte. The luftwafte came over and blew half the company, well the beach group anyway to pieces. Half of them – 50% of them became casualties.

All the lads all lined up there; I think half of the company became casualties. We spoke to some that were coming down and they said, "That sergeant that's with you, was one of the sergeants that made us put our kits out and tents out in lines in a regimental fashion, instead of making us put them out scattered all over the place." – which they should of done. We still had aircraft come over from Sicily.

So I was having a sleep when suddenly I heard bang, bang, bang. These two lads, and there 7 of us in total, had decided to shoot at the Sergeant who had caused the rest of our company to become casualties. That was the fruits of the war; I think that had a big bearing on it as two of the lads were in that company. When we stopped at a railway station we used to let the prisoners out to relieve themselves by the side of the train. They stepped onto the platform and in full view of the rest of the train were marching down and unfortunately the two Liverpool fellows who were well oiled, opened up with their rifles at the Sergeant and it was the funniest sight you ever saw. I don't think that they shot at him to kill him; they shot at him anyway, as I was asleep and it certainly woke me up.

They aimed at the sergeant and you saw him disappear up the line, they couldn't aim properly, well they didn't, but unfortunately for there were two RAF police sergeants at the railway station and they had a good view of them two. When we a couple of lads shot off and we ended up in central nick in Algiers. The funny thing about it was, the two red cap RAF police dived for safety through the station windows, this sergeant that they didn't mean to shoot him took off, left his false teeth behind.

When it was all said and done, and of course the sergeant was missing he had disappeared up the line somewhere. When we got to Algiers there was a huge cordon of police and out train was shunted into a siding and all the escort was put under arrest including myself.

The train was stopped of course at Setief, and the guards were shunting up the line and I have never seen so many red caps in all my life. They were armed to the teeth with Tommy guns, they stormed in "lie down, stick your hands up, and get your arses out of here" and the whole guard was marched off. We were chained together. As we were marched out, all the Italian prisoners were cheering.

They took us to the central police station which was jointly run by British, American and French. We slept on those stone slabs whilst they searched our luggage, and unfortunately they found some money – a lot of money. This was the money that the Germans paid the soldiers for extra luxuries such as cigarettes. What they were after though was not the money but the smell of the guns and we found out that the two guns and their numbers corresponded with the two Liverpool lads. They were then arrested, we arrested as well, but we were allowed out, until the escort came and marched us back. That was the end of escapades with the prisoners, of going back and forwards so we lost a bit of wotsname.

There was no blankets we just laid on the cell floor, and that was Algiers prison. The next cell to us was full of, I am not sure whom they were, but we think they were ones that supported Admiral Delang who was shot.

In my small pack, as my kit bag was back at our unit. I had 5 red devils but they were all disarmed, they were easy to disarm, you could push a pin in and the bottom would come off. Cupped in there was the charge and detonator and it was a little thing on top, which you could pull, which dropped off and fired it, like a rifle. You used to leave it there for when they wanted to turn it into a lighter. This red cap turned white when he was examining my bag. They were all disarmed but the look on his face was a picture. We spent two weeks in jail, for the first two days we had no food and we had no exercise the whole time we there.

The army never liked looting. I never looted it was just stuff that was lying around. The Americans used to buy it, the stuff that the Italians took. That was that. If we saw anything lying around like red devils we could turn them into lighters. Pistols they went over the moon for. Sometimes if you got, I did see one but I never had it myself, it was a pistol that had been given to a German officer at a cadet's school. I wouldn't take stuff off anyone, as they had earnt it the same as everyone else.

Anyway I was innocent. Only two of our lads got court martialled and that was the two Liverpool lads. The funny thing about it was when we left and got our kit, in fact they took off all our bolts off our rifles and they handed them over to an escort. I said, "Who is under escort?" he said, "You will find out when you get back to camp". We didn't go back to camp; we went back to Philipville in that big barracks and that was the court martial centre. We when all went up there were no case to answer, there were 6 of us and the two who did get court martialled. They wanted to call us as witnesses, and I said," I am not a witness I never heard anything and I never saw nothing".

The two lads did own up but the Red Caps could see it was their guns that were still smoking when they surrounded us. They were eventually court martialled and were done for this shooting. I think they were sent to Aden – which was a hellhole of a prison.

In memory of the fact that they came from Liverpool we used to sing Maggie May "Maggie Maggie May, they have taken her away, to some far distant shore, she done so many sailors and took so many sailors, she wont go down Lime street any more."

This explains why we were shooting at our own people that were wrong. They shouldn't have done that. Anyway that seemed to them at the time to be right. I was exonerated. I wasn't one of them but I spent a very uncomfortable couple of weeks in Algiers jail.

We found out we weren't involved and they just said, "Alright you go back to your squadron". The two that were pointed by the two sergeants were held there. We got back to the squadron much to the amazement of our Commander and he said, "I thought you were all in the nick". I said, "We were, they let us as they had nothing on us". "Right", he said, "I am going to give you another little job, and you can go up to the Navy".

I resigned the rank of corporal and returned as a Sapper. The dockyard was making up my money, as I joined between the Munich crisis and the war, when we actually came to the war. During this time became known as the "booby trap king". I handled booby traps, mines and made up charges and explosives give off vapour, that is absorbed by the body into the bones.

By May 1943 – the 5th Panzer Army is destroyed, the 15th Panzer Division surrenders to the 7th Armoured Division. By this time the British had captured 50,000 prisoners. The German 90th Light Division – old enemies of the 8th Army were completed surrounded in its entirety.

Preparation for Pantelleria

There were a few other skirmishes and do's and anyway we saw the armistice of the Germans and we went into a transit camp to re-equip. I should imagine for Pantelleria and Sicily. A lot of men I trained with especially in the UK, not in action, but coming back from Pantelleria. There was a scotch company and he had been recruited from men that worked in the council and that's what some of our ones that I had something to do with. In fact my wife's uncle was in one, I actually saw him three times, once in Africa and once in Sicily, once in Italy.

There were about 8 or 9 of us. They now think we were doing small portions of old mobile Harbour that they used at D-day. They were now getting ready for Pantelleria and of course later on Sicily and what we were doing were building big floating tanks, we were joining together things we had from the Bailey bridge, the bits that rocked up and down. We were near Falco and Suez. We were also learnt the total number of men that had been killed or wounded.

The navy were making these naval pontoons and putting them together. We found out afterwards what they were for, they wanted us to drive our armoured bulldozers and push them into the sea. This was near a place called Philipville. In Philipville we went to, when we finished back to another nasty little thing happened. We were all going through this business of assault landings, we were just finished getting sorted out by the German luftwafte.

We were making out we were landing on the beach. To make it real a couple of Messerschmitts came over and dropped a couple of bombs but they never went off. Of course being engineers, they grabbed us; we fished them out, put them in a landing craft took them out and dropped them that was the quickest way. Next thing the Canadians were firing us at whilst we were under this barbwire, they fired over your heads. It was the princess Patricia's Rifles, they were pretty good shots, they never killed anybody.

Another nasty thing, this happened the next day, we were all in a circle, very bored and a sergeant and a corporal were showing us how to fire a prode from your rifle using a balanite cartridge. So for the balanite cartridge you put the butt of your rifle into the ground and you aim towards where the enemy was and I sitting in the circle just behind the sergeant and there was a terrific explosion and the head of the sergeant just disappeared. I got smothered in little damp drops of what I should imagine his head. There had been a miss-tilt. Anyway we got over that, we used to go swimming everyday along that stretch of beach as well.

Pantallerio 1943

Operation Corkscrew was the capture of an island, Pantallerio. The Tunisian campaign was over and the Italian yet to begin, consequently Corkscrew was neither a 1st Army nor an 8th Army operation but an independent force mounted by Allied Force HQ at Algiers. The result is that Corkscrew has been overlooked in official war histories and very little has been written for the record; and yet the capture of Pantallerio, the first ever conquest of Axis territory, was essential to the forthcoming Sicily landings by denying the Luftwafte use of its airfield thereby opening sea-lanes for the support of the Sicily operation, raising the siege of Malta and opening the passage to India via the Suez Canal. The importance of Pantallerio Island resulted from its location. It was right in the middle of the Mediterranean Sea being 53 miles to the east of Tunisia and 63 miles to the southwest of the island was Sicily.

Considered by many to be an impregnable military fortress, Pantallerio was studded with heavy gun emplacements and well-concealed batteries. Indeed, Aerial reconnaissance over the 42-square mile rock island revealed more than 100 gun emplacements, embedded in rock or concrete. It had a garrison of some 10,000 troops.

The enemy had Freya radio direction finder stations on Pantallerio with enough range to detect Allied planes taking off from North African airfields. Those stations would prevent tactical surprise for any Sicilian invasion. The Island held an estimated eighty German and Italian fighter planes on its Marghana Airfield, along with a number of bombers. Its various coves and grottoes sheltered motor torpedo boats and submarines that would pose a serious threat to an Allied invasion convoy.

So, in the hands of the enemy, Pantallerio constituted a grave menace to our Sicilian operation.

On the other hand, the capture of the Island and its airfield would provide an excellent base for Allied fighters to protect our shipping and to furnish close support for our landing forces on Sicily.

By early May 1943, plans to take Pantallerio had been drawn up under the *code name Operation CORKSCREW. An amphibious assault was set for June 11th*

Even before the enemy surrender in Tunisia on May 13th, Northwest African Air Force (NAAF) attacks began against Pantallerio and continued throughout that month on an increasing scale. Fighter-bombers, mediums and heavies pounded away at the Island's defences.

They began by wrecking the airfield, destroying numerous aircraft on the ground. Then they sank the ships in the harbour. This done, they attacked the gun emplacements one by one. A complete air blockade against supply and reinforcement was accomplished.

Starting June 7th, the aerial attacks went on around the clock and a naval bombardment also began. With the weight of bombs gradually stepped up each day, the NAAF delivered its knockout punch June 10th following the refusal of the Island's garrison to respond to demands for surrender.

That day more bombs were dropped on Pantallerio than had been dropped during the entire month of April on all enemy targets in Tunisia, Sicily, Sardinia and Italy put together. The Army Air Forces official history described how "wave after wave of bombers swept over former Tunisian battlefields and out across the Mediterranean." Observers were "struck by the power of the aerial weapon which the allies had forged."

In the June of 1943 14,203 bombs amounting to 4,119 tons were dropped on 16 batteries. Out of 80 guns bombed 43 were damaged 10 beyond repair. All control communications were destroyed together with many gun emplacements, ammunition stores, air-raid shelters and all the elements of a WW2 artillery system. About an hour before the landing craft reached the beaches the ships opened fire. When the first of the Commandos landed the white flag was already flying. Churchill was to record later in his memoirs that the only casualty was a man bitten by a mule!

At 1100 Hours on the morning of the 11th, with our assault force offshore, a terrific pre-invasion bombing silenced the last of the Island's batteries. A final pounding was delivered to the Pantallerio harbour area. "Suddenly the whole harbour area appeared to rise and hang in midair, while smoke and dust billowed high, dwarfing Montagna Grande, Pantallerio's tallest peak." Soon thereafter, Allied planes spotted a white cross on the airfield. Shortly after noon, Vice Adm. Gino Pavesi, the Military Governor, surrendered Pantallerio and British troops landed unopposed.

The Pantallerio harbour facilities had been badly damaged and the town itself practically destroyed. Water mains were broken, road were obliterated and electricity plus communications were cut off. The Marghana airfield was cratered and except for two aircraft, all of the 80-plus aircraft had been destroyed or damaged.

This air offensive against Pantallerio was the heaviest concentrated bombing, both in weight of explosives and number of sorties, delivered against a single Axis target up to that time. Surrender of the Island, after the aerial assault rising in crescendo had battered it into submission, marked the first instance of strongly defended enemy territory being conquered solely from the air in the absence of an accompanying ground invasion. The precision with which the operation was carried out caused

CORKSCREW to be considered a military classic.

Operation Corkscrew

Pantallerio – June 1943

The next thing was, I was talking about this stone frigate. I forget the name of what was called. What they wanted us for, there were small bulldozers we used to practice on the sand, and then in the sea. The area was marked out of bounds. I think the 51st Division was billeted there. Of course they were all watching us. What we used to do was push a line of these tanks until they were in the water. Well the idea then was that men could run along them and run ashore but then, this is how it happened. These landing craft, the small bulldozes went in first at the far end. Then there was a line of these gantries that went into the sea. They were in lengths of 12 or 14 tanks with the bailey hinges going up and down out at sea. They would then push them off from the landing craft. They then floated and they had to be swung into position and they could be locked together in pairs. These are the ones that came from the Stone frigate.

When then got in to the landing craft and off we went, we all thought we were going to do a little landing at one of the bid islands but then suddenly word went around and it was Pantelleria. At the same time as that was happening – American bombers were flying in very big formations came over and were bombing something on the horizon, which we now know was Pantelleria. When we landed it was like landing on the moon.

The American bombers had left very little standing and I thought this at the time that there could not be very many alive, but I was very much mistaken. I don't think there was a person killed in that total bombardment. Pantelleria just disappeared we thought "Christ there wont be nobody left there". If we had used the flattel tank we would have blown ourselves to bits there bombs that didn't go off that got caught up with the blast and feathered down all over the place. In fact we had to get the American armourers over to tell us how to get these bombs away, which they did. They did it very quickly too. We then occupied the island.

First of all there was no one on the island or so we thought. All the aircraft and everything were destroyed. We heard banging and the steel doors that were locked outside at the hanger. Near what was left of this volcano, and then there they were, thousands of them. We got them all out, sorted them all out, there were women too. They were all taken down to the landing craft and taken, some as prisoners to North Africa.

There was a massive naval presence: Destroyers, HMS Laforey, Jervis, Tartar, Nubian, Loyal, Troubridge, Lookout and Waddon sped here and there as they shepherded the craft to their destination. Four cruisers...HMS Aurora (with General Eisenhower aboard) Newfoundland, Penelope, and Eurylaus, and the river gunboat Aphis, were there awaiting their moment. Up above, the fighters of the RAF glinted in the sunlit sky as they patrolled the airspace.

The first wave of assault craft landed at 12 on 11th June 1943, with the rest of the Division landing in the following hours. 248 Field Company formed part of the assaulting force. By late afternoon, the commanding Italian Admiral had surrendered the island.

Actually the landing was such that nobody was hurt, there was people killed later but not then. Well we were shoved off, attached to each other with troops on. They went alongside and off went these troops onto these jetties; then run ashore quite dry. Before all this had happened, the American air force, in fact these planes came from the same place as the Red caps, British air force, that saw the two men shoot at the sergeant at a place called Setief.

I never have seen so many bombs come down in all my life. We went ashore and there was lire blowing around – the Americans hit a bank.

Blowing around was lire notes. The bank had been blown up and there was lire blowing around and all the lads were collecting this for souvenirs. We then got our bulldozers out, our section was a GB section we used to have scorpion tanks for destroying mines which were not needed and bulldozers which were needed to make these paths. One of the Americans had dropped in on the bank or the post office and there was all the money for the troops in Libya. We collected some and after a few days I was a lire millionaire. After about 4 or 5 days they were picking these things up for souvenirs we had to look very carefully to make sure no one had wiped their arse on it! Everyone tried to pocket some but we went for the notes with the bigger numbers. We later found out the ones with lower numbers were worth more.

This episode happened and I don't know why, the Italian submarine stuck in my mind. We were being visited by the luftwafte, fortunately for us the defenders of these islands, left all the anti- aircraft guns, more or less active, none of them had been destroyed. So when the luftwafte came over we could just dive onto these guns and belt off at them. That used to put them off. One day instead of the luftwafte come, an Italian submarine came up. Put his flag up and shelled at the island and they hit a sort of a lighthouse. The RAF Red caps occupied the lighthouse; I think 6 or 7 were killed. We jumped on these guns and started firing. We could see some of the bullets bouncing off. Down it went, and then it was gone, before the Navy could go up there with the depth charges. Up come the navy with depth charges going off left right and centre but nothing happened. I don't think they sank it.

On the island we found a large storeroom with massive steel doors. Cut it

145

open with acetylene torch and found lots of equipment, including 12 berrete pistols, which I then pocketed, and also lots of typewriters, none of which had been used.

The Italian garrisons on other nearby islands (Linosa and Lampedusa) quickly fell. This cleared the way for the invasion of Sicily a month later.

Then we were going back. We went back on one of these very large landing craft. Very nearly the whole of the garrison could fit on this one, including a lot of my mates that was in the company of Scotland. They were from Paisley and they were in a field company, 1st Infantry division, which I later joined as well. A lot of them became casualties. When leaving the island it was getting dusk, and was just getting something to eat when I saw the bow suddenly go right up with an explosion. We were just sailing along, when BANG. Up went the bows and down went the ship. We all scrambled out and were shortly picked up. The landing craft disappeared. In fact to make this record I wrote a letter to the navy records and they couldn't find anything about this blinking ship. It was a ghost ship anyway. Anyway that went down, we got picked up and a few days after that we were on our way to Sicily. Quite a lot of the lads from that Scots company were recruited from Paisley, and they were from the government or the council. A lot of them became casualties. Eventually we got picked up but unfortunately too our collectables in our white's car was at the bottom of the drink.

The tragedy was just outside Sousse harbour. The ship with 238 Field Company R (this is the field company that Fred was attached to temporarily for this mission), aboard hit a sea-mine killing or drowning 17 and wounding several others. The "postie" distinguished himself beyond the call of duty by braving the incoming waters to rescue his mail bags from the hold to secure what is most precious to the soldier - his mail.

After we got fished out we went to Sousse. The old man said "Blimey you do like trouble, anyway there is a little job going down at Philipville." He says "Keep out of bloody prison". We couldn't see the two lads that were in there. We did eventually see them but later on.

After the successful capture of Pantallerio, the 1st Division returned to North Africa where they were held in reserve and trained for mountain warfare. Everyone was given 5 days leave. Various rest camps had been set up by the Division on the coast, where men could relax, bathe, enjoy canteen facilities and the occasional film show.

After getting kitted up and cleaned up we went to pick up some new white cars and dingoes. On the way back from the depot in Egypt we stopped at a transit camp in Sinai. This happened on the border between Egypt and Palestine in the Sinai desert. This is the beginning of the lion story. The lion cub had been found by the South Africans when they liberated Abyssinia under General Schmitz. There was a South African Cape Town rifles or something in occupation there getting grub. We pulled in, we had a dog and he didn't half start growling.

Jimmy Hardman front left with the dog

I said "what's he growling about?" Then suddenly out of the big marquee came a lion, a full grown African Lion. It appeared that the South Africans had found it as a cub and brought it up, it was now fully grown and they had it as a mascot. It looked like it was boss eyed but he just growled at the dog. He seemed to be used to dogs and fortunately one of our lads had a spare can of corn beef. He opened it up and put half down for the lion, and blimey the lion swallowed it in five gallops', and it was a pretty big tin too.

The story of this is later when we were going to Sicily, the South Africans and the Australians, and everybody had to put all their animals (as we were going into Europe) apart from Army Dogs, into the zoo. This lion went into the Tel Avis Zoo. The story now revolves after we went through Sicily and Italy and came back. Prior we think to Japan. There was a huge convoy of South Africans came over from Italy, the first thing they did was they went down to the zoo, and they got the lion out (laughing). Once they got it out, he run amok, I think they had to finish him off and shooting it. That was the story before we went to Sicily and when we came back from Italy.

Letter received from Home

This was received by Fred from home telling him of some important news.

July 13th 1943

Tuesday

My own darling Husband & Sweetheart,

I wanted to send a telegram with the news, sweet but there's no service to North Africa, so I guess this is the quickest way of letting you know that you are now the proud father of a bonny son. Yes, Fred, he arrived, last evening at 5.45 and he weighs 7 ½ lbs and talk about being a Britt. Your mother took one look at him and went into a fit where she says he's so much like you darling. And he's not the only that thinks it either my own. I can see you as plain as anything. I think he'll be fair Fred; his eyelashes are so blond you can't see them yet. Darling I wish you could see him. At the present moment he is asleep in his cot (my mistake he has just yelled out and has he some lungs). Anyway he had mum walking the floor with him half the night. (By the way that's your job Fred)

I was in pain since last Friday, dear, so I guess that made it seem worse, but they say it's a pain you soon forget. It was like going through hell while it lasted darling, but he is worth it. Now that he's here and I've held him in my arms, I can see you, sweet. He's worth everything I went through. The nurse said I was a brick and did everything right as she told me, so that went a long way to help, Fred. She was very good, dearest, and made me laugh when I wanted to cry. Jean went down for her at quarter to five. Nurse said she would come back at five when she left for dinner hour but I couldn't wait <u>quite</u> that long. I had to send for her and although she didn't think the baby would arrive until later she was going to stay with me. But it was over at 5.45 and was I surprised and glad when it was Fred?

Charlie has just come in to see his nephew. He's so thrilled as anything Fred, as you can imagine. He brought up a £1 worth of 5d pieces for Alan and your mum gave him 32. Auntie Lil put in 5/- in his hand. She came back after dinner and stayed until it was all over. They shoved me in a hot bath less than four hours before he was born. It's a new idea they have to help you and I believe it does too, though I didn't at the time though this was when I was in so much pain, Fred. The nurse wouldn't allow mum or any one in the room at the time, for she said it's not right for mothers to see their daughters suffering. I always thought I'd like mum to be with me but when the actual time came I told her o go out of the room for I didn't want her to see me like that.

Tony & Brenda can't get over it and if Tony gets half a chance he's up here like a shot, to see the baby. Well, sweetheart, I've just had my dinner. Yesterday I had a cup of tea after it was over, and after that an egg and milk custard and a cup of ovaltine. They never used to give you anything to eat for 3 days, but now you're allowed anything you fancy. I'm not supposed to have visitors for 3 days, dear, but I've had mum and Charlie up. Besides these indoors here only if someone comes we'll have to let them see me when Jean isn't here or she'll go down and tell the nurse. Well, Fred, I'm glad that's it's all over and that everything went off as it did. I didn't need a doctor anyway. I bet you'll be glad to know too sweet. I wish I could have sent a telegram, but they said at the Post Office I could send to your unit and get a concession form and then they would let you know. But mum said she thought this way would be just as quick time we finished sending the form backwards and forwards. Well, sweetheart, I guess this is all for now, so I'll close sending all my fondest love & kisses, tons of love from our baby Alan. Forever your devoted faithful wife Iris, PS Even when I'm looking at him I can hardly believe he is our very son, Darling. I adore you. Darling.

Sousie 1943 – the boots

We went swimming one day and I got a new pair of boots. I got two new pairs of boots actually but my old boots was very comfortable but very very old. When I got married, I got married in them. I went right through Africa and I was now getting ready we know now to go to Sicily. So there were six of us went down swimming, when we come up the beach we took our boots off of course when we went swimming. The camp was not very far from the beach and then we had a little ceremony. We dug a bloody great big slit trench and we buried all the boots. They were very comfortable boots, I cut the eyelets out and they are on a chain. When I did come home and worked in the dockyard I fitted one of them to my chain on my key ring. We buried them in a line; there were six of them, six pairs of boots. We buried them. The camp was only a few yards from where the beach was where we buried them, and we went back with no boots on.

Now we QM's gave us new gear, as we knew we were getting new gear. We hoped we were going home, but we weren't it was Sicily and Italy and then back to the Middle

155

East. We told him about our boots and so the Quarter Master said "that will be less for me to bundle up and send back" so that was that.

We went further into North Africa for training. A section of us then went down with the Navy to Philipville, and we started building these jetties – pontoons, which could go out alongside landing craft and we found out this later on. There was a Naval base where we were making these landing ramps for Sicily. We had to push them into the sea and make sure they were up and down with the tide. We had to allow the infantry to get ashore dry. In fact we saw one tested, and so we knew something was going to come up. After a couple of weeks of this when then moved to the location with our squadron, and prepared for the big one. We went to Bonne to get into our landing craft and then we were taken to Malta. We unloaded at Malta in the dark, and then proceeded to get fed, equipped and told where we were going to go. We were formed in what they call bricks. This is a small division, infantry, engineers, tanks; you name it that was in it.

Personal Message from the Army Commander

"There must be NO withdrawal and no surrender, smash the enemy attack and cause him such casualties it will cripple him. We will give him a very bloody nose. It will be our turn to attack him. Let us show him what the famous Eighth Army can do. Good luck to each one of you and good hunting. BL Montgomery. General GO CinC 8th Army."

Invasion of Sicily

10th July 1943 – Sicily invaded and captured Syracuse. Severe fighting in the east of Sicily, Germans fought hard and using parachutists as infantry. Italians surrendering in their 100's, by the 17th August 1943 resistance ended. As troops entered the main towns were greeted by inhabitants giving water, brandy, figs, and lemons and bunch of grapes.

Operation Husky, the Allied codename for the Anglo-American invasion of Sicily, was mounted to capture Sicily. The operation was under the supreme command of the American Lieutenant General Dwight David Eisenhower (1890-1969). His deputy was the British Lieutenant General Harold Alexander (1891-1969), who commanded the 15th Army Group comprising of the American 7th Army (Patton) and the British 8th Army (Montgomery).

On the night of 9/10 July 1943 the British 1st Airborne Division's glider borne forces (with 9th Airborne Field Company, Royal Engineers) began the invasion with the capture of the Ponte Grande bridge south of

Syracuse and on the morning of 10 July 1943 the ground troops of the British 8th Army landed on the beaches between Cassabile and Castellazo.

The plan required the Divisional engineers to:

- *Deal with beach obstacles and minefields below and above high water mark.*
- *Prepare tracks up and exits off the beaches.*
- *Repair or construct airfields.*
- *Facilitate the advance inland.*

Sicily was conquered in 38 days during which time the engineers constructed 38 Bailey and 20 Small Box Girder (SBG) bridges, in addition to a number of causeways, minor bridges and roads repairs. The airfield construction groups prepared 16 fair weather airfields. The Railway units operated the railway at Syracuse and established a railhead in support of the advancing troops. The Port units took over the repair and operation of the ports of Syracuse, Augusta, Catania, Messina and Milazzo.

The Allied invasion of Sicily in July 1943, codenamed Operation Husky, was highly successful, although many of the Axis forces there were allowed to avoid capture and escape to the mainland. More importantly a coup deposed Benito Mussolini as head of the Italian government, which then began approaching the Allies to make peace. It was believed a quick invasion of Italy might hasten an Italian surrender and produce quick military victories over the German troops that would now be trapped fighting in a hostile country.

Before crossing the river Simeto found the enemy in considerable strength on the Mt Etna Line.

After Sicily was secured it was possible for the Allies to use it as a springboard to invade Italy. The Anglo-American force, 15th Army Group, under General Harold Alexander (1981-1969) consisting of the American 5th Army (Clark) and the British 8th Army (Montgomery) began their invasion on 9 September 1943. The invasion plan was for a three-prong attack at the selected points of Salerno, Reggio and Taranto. The latter two were carried out by the 8th Army and were met with little or no opposition. The Americans at Salerno met with stiff opposition but did eventually manage to secure a beachhead.

After the Salerno beachhead had been secured the American 5th Army advanced up the west side of Italy while the British 8th Army advanced up the east. Each army had to batter its way north through a series of well prepared German defence - Viktor Line, Gustav Line, Caesar Line, and Gothic Line. Progress was slow hampered by the mountainous terrain, with its sheer faces, steep gullies and false crests coupled with deep valleys of marshes and broad rivers. The engineers were used extensively to overcome these obstacles.

We now got ready for Sicily and we went off, got our boats and went across the water to Malta first. I think we were there for at least three days, there we were pretty well entertained, they certainly looked after us, and with us from the 1st Infantry Division was a Scotch battalion. We were all in a RAF place and a lot of the bigwigs came down and were talking to us, wishing us all god speed as everyone knew we were going to go. This colonel said, "That the first gun we capture we will send back to Malta", and he did. My brother went to Malta along time after the war and when he said this he was taken to the British legion, well the Maltese legion place and the fellow in charge showed him the gun. Since then my brother and a couple of mates from the club have been over there and saw it.

We were now on the way to Malta and then on to Sicily. We went across and landed at a place called Syracuse. I think I have said this before about the Mafia, we didn't know what it was. They called themselves Mafioso. We were told we need to meet a guide and the guide was one of these and he was a youngster. He was a soldier of the Mafioso and he was to lead us to wherever we wanted to go. They guided us to minefields and to where the Germans were. There were Italians ready to pack in. In one place they went into field up this road and there very nearly was a whole regiment of coast defence Italians ready to pack in and they were just waiting for us. So we had to come and take them. In fact they just went back to the beach where we were. I think they put them on clearing mines.

Prior to the landing there these Navy Landing ships with all these rockets on and they more or less blew a path for us when we got ashore the first thing we saw was this concrete bunkers. All you could see was the iron in the concrete, the concrete was bare and then suddenly this youngster comes up and they had red buffers so you could distinguish them. This Mafioso came up and said in quite good English – American – English, he was actually a yank. We asked how he spoke so good English and he said "Well I was born in America but unfortunately my father was deported". Of course the wife and the children went with him.

He was only a tiny child then but he learnt English. Another thing was English was a pretty good language to learn in Sicily or Italy. That is how he started, but he led us right through from Syracuse to Augusta, from Augusta to the University City where the Germans were really hold up. I think he spent most of his time picking up schmizzers, by the time he finished with us he had ten schmizzers. I don't know what we wanted them for.

All the British troops were now pushing forward towards Catania. This was a university town and it was held by our old friends from the desert the 90th Light, and they knew how to fight, mind you so did we, I mean we did win the bloody war!

It took us about eight or nine days to subdue the Germans in Catania Before we could move onto the capital of Sicily, Palermo. We had to battle all our way there; there were minefields and there was an airfield there. The one little thing that bothered us there was the German dogs we managed to see one of the last planes off which was a big Junkers. They were trying to pull the dogs up. These were the guard dogs of course once they got off and they headed for Italy, the dogs were just left there. They didn't go much on us; they were trained to more or less have a go at the uniform. We had to shoot them and I didn't like seeing that.

The next thing was we had to check through the airfield and we found in one hanger when we were clearing it for booby traps and mines, there was an Airspeed envoy. It was strapped to the wall so it probably had no parts in there. They were built in Portsmouth.

Also there was that little episode when we found the big glider full up with the Staffs, Staffordshire Regiment and they had all drowned. It appeared when they cut them off to land in Sicily, they landed on the sea, and it turned over. We had the job of dragging this glider up the beach. We lined the men all out, they had all been dead for as long as the island had been fighting because they were coming in on the night before. All the men in there drowned and we had to carry them up the beach and the grave recognition unit was identifying and burying the dead. When we cleared all the equipment out we found these bags with the sten guns in. They had been assembled and I got one then. I kept one of them. The rest of the stuff was piled up and then ordnance came and got it.

We carried up explosives we found on the beach, we do small explosions. We had to dig a hole in and then run the bulldozer over. The big stuff we into Mount Etna and blew them up. Certain things happened. We just cleared the stuff away, we fired off this lot and there was a terrific great bang. Then a swarm of British, German, Italian soldiers came out of the catacombs which were out of Etna. They thought the volcano was going to explode on them.

Before crossing the river Simeto we found the enemy in considerable strength on the Mt Etna line. Eventually we succeeded and the 90th Light managed to mostly get out of Sicily. We caught a lot of them and of course when we went to Palermo, the Americans just beat us to it. Of course they had an easier run than we did. The American 5th Army got there before we did. I mean we did have a bit of a ding-dong but it didn't matter about who won first prize, Sicily was now captured. I think that got up Montgomery's snout. In any case he was still our commander; we now planned for Regio Del Cabria, which we could see from Palermo across the straits.

Old Monty was making a great TISWAS about being the first troops back into Europe which I don't think anyone realised now that we were. The day came and over we went.

We did see one of our cruisers go down, it was a mine layer and I think she was sweeping for mines in that channel. Big bang and we just looked we saw the tail end going down; I am not sure what the name was, although I can remember as I used to work in the yard – dockyard. We went across the channel and our first task was Taranto. Off we shot towards Taranto. There were a few Germans but they were mostly Italians shouting "Long live us" and God knows what else.

Invasion of Italy

Anyway this we got ready for our next little trip across the sea. We went across to the Straits of Messina and followed the main road to Taranto. We landed after the usual barrage. Montgomery loved his barrages! As we stormed ashore there was nobody there apart from this poor little Old Italian woman sitting in a chair outside of her house and she had an apron over her head. I don't know what that was going to save her from! Anyway it did as we went up past she was singing the praises of the British soldiers and along we went.

Just before we were ready for that, I am not sure on the dates, a couple of days. The cruiser that was mine laying there and hit something and went down. I think most of the men got off. Italy then of course was an unknown quantity. As far as we were concerned Italy was the enemies they had done a few shove offs and done a few air raids before we went across. We went across and the two armies then split it was the 5th Army, which I eventually went to, and the 8th, which I was in.

The 8th went right across to the straits. The 5th Army waited a few days and went up towards Salerno and to Naples. This landing was to draw off the Germans from down where were, which they did. When we got ashore at Reggio Del Calabria we went straight across and followed the toe and up towards the Adriatic side. Now there was something very nasty that happened. We heard over the blower that troops had got ashore at Salerno on the way round we heard they ran into trouble. So what happened then a couple of our brigades moved across to the centre of Italy.

We tried to take some pressure off the troops ashore at Salerno and were moving across Italy to help them. The notable exception was the lad that I used to sit aside at the Roman Catholic school In Portsmouth we had to leave behind. We got pretty far advanced when we got over and as we dropped back to the beaches we had to leave some of our wounded behind. Our Roman Catholic priest stayed with them. His name was Hutchings they were taken prisoner and they went up to Poland in the coal mines.

At Taranto there was the Italian Navy, now I don't know if the soldiers get any prize money but the navy do, but who did capture the bloody fleet? Was it the Army or the Navy, no sign of sailors there saw plenty of soldiers - that's something for the history books. We went on and it weren't until Bari when we heard about this mutiny at Salerno. We started to come across but unfortunately the Americans had made such a good job of bombing Foggia that was it! We couldn't get through then we heard that the Salerno beachhead had broken out and we were on a way to Naples.

The main thing in Taranto Harbour we could see the Italian Harbour and we put guards on them and took them back to Malta. We then dashed onto I think it was Bari. It was not too bad to cross the rivers quite easily; it wasn't until later that we had some trouble. The worst ones were the Trigno and later on Sangro. That was a terrible battle. At Bari we suddenly heard about the trouble that these troops were having at Salerno.

For the first time there were fields of tomatoes. Of course the lads couldn't resist walking through and eating them and it wasn't the Germans who would defeat us it was the fruit. Tomato plantations and god knows what else and they stuffed themselves and they got the runs. A lot of them got typhoid and malaria. We had more casualties with malaria and guts ache, including me but that was a bit later. We had more fruit that we could have eaten, eat or kept, or carry and so loaded up our Lorries.

We pulled on past Taranto I think it was Foggia. The people at Salerno had forced their way out of the beach head and were heading towards Naples. So we now turned around and we went back the route we were going towards Pescara. So instead of going up towards on the Adriatic side and then we heard about the mutiny at Salerno. This was only bush telegraph then and I can say something more about later. It was something like this; cruisers had gone to Africa and picked up the ones that had come out of hospital. They were in a transit camp. They were members of the 50th and 51st, 8th Army crack divisions. They were rushed across the med to Salerno but when they got there it had sorted itself out.

Now this was another nasty episode. There was bombers coming over and they literally flattened Foggia I don't know the reason as according to the people in Foggia the Italian Army and the German Army had pulled out. The number of bombers that went over there well it was devastated the place, in fact it made blasted hard for us to get through. We had to go right into the country side and try and get round as the streets were now one big mass of rubble. The Americans had bombed it and all the roads were impossible to get through. We had to get through and try and clear it. It was of course there was a few die hard Germans in there sniping away. We heard that everything was normal at Salerno, and that the 5th Army – where the Hampshire Brigade was, had now recovered and were heading towards Naples. So we about turned and went on our normal rout. We got around it and the next place was Bari, and we kind of came across to Bari.

Our next port of call was Taranto and as you will know we caught the Navy there, the Italian Navy that is. Where the Italian Navy were ready to surrender, they were all hanging out their white flags. It was a funny little harbour Taranto, I thought it would be a huge place but there was a bridge going across and our tanks went up to the bridge and the Italians put it back in position and away we went onto and up to the Bari coast up along there. I think we branched off into Foggia and that was in a terrible condition. It had really been bombed it was something like Berlin.

Now on the way to Taranto I got some funny tummy pains and I found out that I had to look at someone and I used to go to toilet. This was from all the fruit and everything that I had been eating. Anyway we went to the quack and he told us that we shouldn't have eaten too much tomatoes and wotnot's. Now at this particular time the American 5th Army, which I wasn't in then, I was still in the 8th, they had landed at a place called Salerno, and they were finding it very, very tough. So on the way back to Sicily General Hospital that was me with this guts ache, I thought I would go to North Africa as most troops that had caught guts ache did do but the General Hospital had come from North Africa and was now in Sicily. Well I spent 4 or 5 days before I started getting cleaned up and towards the end they said that as I was now more or less on my feet that I could do a bit of duty.

The chap in charge of the unit where we were recuperating from, we come out of the hospital was, said "you got to do something so you may as well as do something whilst you are here". That unit there is going to move over to the mainland, what we didn't know; not very far from us was a detention centre.

Salerno Mutiny – September 1943

So four of us went to a recording were the telephone section was for the 8th army and I learnt something to my disadvantage there. First of all we would get all the calls, in charge of us was this corporal of the engineers who was on python, which was meant that he had done his turn abroad and he waiting to go home.

We heard some very funny things. Suddenly we heard the Salerno Mutiny. This comes off the radio from a detention quarters, which was on Sicily that was getting in touch with North Africa. That had some more men coming over and this is what appeared happened. I don't know if it is true as there were four men talking about from two different places and a third man, this was on the telephone, came in on it. The first two had pronounced Scots accents or north accents and they appeared to be the commanders of detention centres one in Sicily one in North Africa. They were saying 200 men had refused to join the units other than the units they had been wounded in, which was the 50th and 51st and that sat on their haversacks. They were going to be charged with mutiny, I think it was over 300, 300 something; anyway, eventually some of the men went to the units and went to the Salerno.

The fifth army was then on its way up towards Naples. Of course they wanted these men to join the 5th Army but they were 8th Army. There was also this nasty thing that the 50th and 51st were going to go home to the second front. Most of the soldiers that were in charge there were from the 8th Army but the silly buggers in charge said no have got to join these units. Well they said right, they put their tools down and that's as far as we heard then.

This was now a precarious position or so it said I don't think we were but anyway there was panic stations and although we were in the hospital we were more or less told that there were a lot of troops coming over from hospitals in North Africa, and they were to reinforce the Salerno Landing. There was one little mistake there, most of the troops that were coming over had been wounded were sick or were sent from North Africa had come from the two North Divisions.

Now this is what we heard. Somebody wrote it down not me, I have got to say that as there is thing called the Official Secrecy act, I shall try and put it together, and it was this. The two voices were officers of course but were North Country and one appeared to be the detention commander and the other one was a reinforcement depot and it was something like this. I haven't got room for over 300 bodies you will have to take them back if you are going to charge them. The voice from North Africa said, "I am not all that keen on this blinking wotsname, none of the senior officer's likes this"; "well I can't handle them," said the one in Sicily.

Well I never thought much more about this the bodies the word bodies in the wotsname. I was under the impression that bodies were troops that had been killed but these were mutineers or so they said. It was a stupid thing as first of all I don't believe in mutiny but this was such a silly one.

Unfortunately most of the best divisions and a lot of the senior officers were going home to the second front. The 50th and the 51st and the 7th Armoured, and a lot of independent brigades. They all went home

177

because of their experience of landings. These men at Salerno had come from Africa. They were wounded and they came from these divisions that were going to go home. Of course bush telegraph said and that was generally right, these divisions were going home, but these men were being posted to division that had just come out of the UK and so they didn't think much on it. So they downed tools and sat on them.

We later found out, it was the British North Divisions, the 51st Highlanders and the, we used to called them the Island Decorators, they used to have marvellous signs all over the place, I think they were the only unit in the army that done it, and the 50th the Tees and Tynes, and when they landed in Sicily, prior to what they thought was their unit. They were then suddenly told they were going to reinforce units in Salerno. Well they downed tools and what I am going to say now influenced, well, didn't influence me but I was quite sympathetic to them.

The main cause was this Montgomery had told the 8th Army units the 51st and the 50th that they were going to home and that were to be used on the landings on D-Day.

Anyway they sat on their knapsacks and said "no we are not going", they were given warnings. As I said before the 50th and 51st were two of the top divisions in the 8th Army.

Anyway we heard no more from it and I tried to find out more. We went to the main land as I was on that particular job for about 4 or 5 days and then I went back to my own unit where I heard just after I left the division or brigade had started to move across to Salerno. The other thing was this when I got back to my unit I found out that the Salerno landing had progressed to plan and they were on the way to Naples. Our lot, the 7th Armoured Brigade, were on its way to off to, they couldn't get to Foggia but we had to go down farther and cross into Bari. So we then moved on our forward motion on the Adriatic coast.

The next thing was I went back to my unit I was in Bari when the next part came out and we looked in the 8th Army news and we looked in the Crusader and me and my mates and none of us could see it and they started thinking that I was telling a wotsname but we had some of these notes down on a signal pad, and most of them copied it, I had one, but the bit that interested me of course was the bodies, where they said bodies. That never bothered me until later.

Rivers - Italy

Any river became a defensive struggle. It was heavily mined but the Germans never held near the bank. They always withdrew back, the only difference that I could remember was Rapido, Nettuno, Trigno and Sangro, that was when they defended from the bank which made it bloody awkward to get across. Anyway most of the other rivers were small and they withdrew right back and relied on mines. In fact in the last stage before the Italian Partisans caught Mussolini he only held the high hills, the side hills were heavily mined and of course he caught in cross fire, no Germans in the middle and mines in the middle, cross fire of artillery and this made it awkward to get through.

I mentioned the partisans quite a lot and these came into the British Army after the occupation. The army went guerrilla and they were announced as partisans and also the partisans of Yugoslavia. A lot of partisans were getting shot as soon as they got captured by the Italians that were loyal to Mussolini. So Field Marshall Alexander said that the partisans were members of the allied forces and they had to wear a red symbol and officers had to wear florenzi. I still have got one from the Italian partisan when I was wounded. The Germans then ceased to shoot them and treat them like the partisans in Russia, which was as soon as they were caught they were shot. Of course we done very well but these men behind the Germans and they used to let us know what the Germans were up to and where the mines were.

Volturno river crossing

The first river crossing was the worst. It was the Volturno. Although the 4th Armoured Brigade was marked for the far side of the river in Italy, we had to come across and help the rest of the 7th Armoured. The landing at Salerno, which we found out, was alright and they were on their way to Naples. Topure was where our brigade was and we manage to get across the river. Unfortunately the only bridge that was being used, as we were further up than the others, was a wooden structure which would never take tanks. We did manage to get a small bulldozer over and that managed to level the bank on the far side as well as our side for a bailey bridge. We then started clearing the mines but we were under fire. Before we managed to get the gaps done properly we had to dispose of these, I think it was the KR's mechanised infantry, and they had come across with their Bren carriers and put them out.

Our tanks were CLY; they soon made a mess of the far bank – that's the Germans. We then stopped and pushed on to allow the other troops going towards Naples. We now went across to the Bari side and we went onto the next river crossing.

Of course the rain that was falling, it may not have been down where you were but it was up in the mountains and it would come down towards the sea. It made things rather hard. Typical of the Germans, the Germans always held back off the river and they did this in Normandy later on. There was always machine gun fire.

This concerns a port called Termoli; we invaded this from the main part of the army.

It was 2 commandos, five of our tanks and a squadron of our sappers. We went ashore and cleared the beaches, and the tanks come up behind us. We occupied the town; there was little opposition the enemy was taken by surprise. Until about the second night and then the Germans attacked but I think they thought we were a bigger force than we were. We captured the port in tact. After about three or four days the Navy came up to us.

Italy - The slog northwards

Throughout the Italian campaign the British, Dominion and Indian engineers were engaged in maintaining, building and repairing roads, constructing bridge and ferry crossings over fast flowing rivers, clearing mines and other obstacles, restoring electricity and water supplies, building troop accommodation, repairing and operating ports and railways, constructing and repairing airfields, mapping, bomb disposal, controlling troop and store movements, and maintaining the mail services.

On September 16th, orders were received for the brigade, less 111 Field Regiment RA, to move to Taranto: the Brigade Commander went in advance to report to 5 Corps to get the form. All tanks and tracked vehicles were to move by sea and the wheels by ferry from Messina, thence by road to Taranto. Brigade HQ arrived at Taranto on 23rd September and received orders to move to Bari area and come under command 78 Division, being prepared next day to take command of forward reconnaissance elements of the division.

The Desert Rats (7th Armoured Division) have since June 1940 fought their way from Egypt three times across Cyrenaica as far as El Agheila on last occasion pushing to Tripoli, the Mareth Line. They have been fighting the Axis armies at this point for three and a half years.

The force consisted of A Squadron The Royals, one squadron of the Sharpshooters, one squadron 56 Recce Regiment, recce squadron of 1 Air Landing Brigade, one company of 1 Kensington's, 17 Field Regiment RA less one battery, SAS squadron and a similar body known as "Popski's Private Army". 626 Field Squadron RE joined the Force by bits and pieces and subsequently became part of the brigade.

This force had just captured Canosa and was meeting opposition across the River Ofanto, over which the bridge was blown: on the coast the town of Barletta was not yet occupied. Very little progress was made this day, but Barletta was finally entered and passed: 4th Armoured Brigade now became the spearhead of the Eighth Army in its advance up the east coast of Italy.

With the Salerno beachhead secure, the 5th Army could begin to attack northwest towards Naples. The 8th Army had been making quick progress from the 'toe' in the face of German engineer delaying actions and linked with the 1st Airborne Division on the Adriatic coast. It united the left of its front with the 5th Army's right on 16 September, and advancing up the Adriatic coast captured the airfields near Foggia on 27 September. Foggia was a major Allied objective because the large airfield complex there would give the Allied air forces the ability to strike new targets in France, Germany and the Balkans. The 5th Army captured Naples on 1 October, and reached the line of the Volturno River on October 6th. This provided a natural barrier, securing Naples, the Campainian Plain and the vital airfields on it from counterattack.

On 3rd November the battle of the River Trigno began. In a hard morning's fighting 46th Royal Tanks lost 7 tanks, accounting for 6 enemy tanks and 2 SP guns. Meanwhile from the ridge south of the Trigno, at least 20 enemy tanks and SP guns had been seen coming down the road from Vasto to San Salvo. They were accurately engaged. In the *afternoon the Brigade Commander was sent for by the Army Commander and ordered to bring 44th Royal Tanks from Serracapriola and take charge of the armoured battle.*

In November 1943 Major ELH Smith was in charge, the 626 Field Squadron suffered from severe weather throughout winter. By the 21st November they were involved in Battle of Sangro and found at least eighty mines and created two tank crossings in a few days.

Extensive reconnaissance of the River Sangro and the ground immediately beyond it were made, but the weather was against us from the start: every time the ground showed signs of drying, down came the rain again, upsetting all precious plans. Meanwhile both divisions had been pushing elements across the River and the brigade was ordered to infiltrate tanks across. 2 KRRC, now under command of 8 Indian Division, had been ordered to occupy Mt Calvo on 15 November: After six very uncomfortable days there, they were ordered to attack and capture the "Castle" feature on the left of the escarpment held by 8 Indian Division. This was a strong and difficult position, well defended with dug-in positions: though they failed in the first attempt, they made no mistake the second time.

The rain kept falling and the river rose at times to such heights and the current to such strength that it was quite unfordable: as a result supply of those troops across the river became most difficult. Bridges were built under most difficult conditions. The first tanks across were of 50th Royal Tanks on 21 November, followed by 9 tanks of Sharpshooters on 22 November. Later a better crossing further up the river was found, but it was not until 28 November that a total of 124 tanks were across.

17th November 1943 – Fred sent a Xmas card home to his family living at 14 Wilson Road. "To my son for his first Xmas from his loving dad"

Card to Fred's son Alan

Minefield Problems

We were clearing a minefield and the officer that was in charge of went forward, we came to a big hole that we had blown and there were mines all round it. We didn't discover the mines as they were all buried until we bought the armoured bulldozer up to fill it in. We used to sling ammunition crates and anything we could get into it, then just run over it and flatten it. Had we done that it would have blown its bloody tracks off. We found these made up charges as the earth came down, I could see them as I was on the other side of this crater. I shouted "stop, stop, stop" pulled him back and I went down there and there were made up charges about five of them.

Another funny little thing happened I wanted to do a wee after we had got these charges out and disarmed them. We stacked them at the side and put them against a wall and also a very small head came up off the wall and he put his hand out and was saying "mines, mines" and pointing down. Sure enough the whole area just wide enough from where I was standing to do a wee were shoe mines. Of course they were buried I couldn't seem them. So I dug them out but you had to be very careful and I was about to say about this officer.

He had gone forward and he was checking some mines, which were shoe mines on the side of the road, and as he picked one up he must have pushed it down, it was like a mouse trap and as you pushed it down the pin would come out and of course away it went. It blew both his hands off. He staggered back and I saw him running backwards and forwards across the road, I went up to him and I could see what had happened. We got hold of him and led him back. We put him on a bulldozer and the bulldozer led him back. We filled the crater in by hand with shovels we slung in a lot of ammunition crates in because we used to bring up a lot then. When we sort of levelled it off we when on forward to try and pick up our infantry, which was the Beds & Herts. – The Bedfordshire and Hertfordshire regiment.

We then went in to billet area, we went down and another infantry regiment, I think it was the Royal Scots came up and went passed and went forward.

In the main us OR's used to stick together. One said something and the others would always agree. There was an old saying about hold your fire and up you I am alright. That applied to all of us. Going up now to Pescara, between Pescara and us was the Sangro and we had to get over that. We were told not to go on the rout to Pescara; the Canadians were going to Pescara.

We moved back to where we had cleared the mines and we found our own unit. Our own unit was now waiting to come through to the sea not that far we headed towards Volturno and then onto another main road that cut across, we were now with our brigade. We now pushed onto our main objective. Our next objective was, we could see the church and the steeple but had not come under fire. The road blocks were Italian carts and broken down Lorries. Most of them were booby trapped. In front of them was craters, and we started filling them in. We used some of the walls on the sides of the roads. We then pushed onto the next and we used the armoured bulldozer to push the cars out of the way. You had to check underneath them to make sure that the ones we did clear didn't blow the tracks off the bulldozer.

After taking this village, now the Italians were given us a hard time. There was this one woman which it had appeared they had shot her husband – he wasn't doing what they were telling him. She showed us where the Germans were hiding. One of our tanks came up once it had been cleared of mines. They blew this strong point up well it was only a house but unfortunately they blew the house to pieces to make sure the Germans had left, and they did very hurriedly.

We then carried on pass this village. There was a long road now and you could see the target, but you could also hear the opposition. To our left that was the ones that had gone across the Volturno. We now saw the German air force and we hadn't seen it before. They came over and went up this road. All the troops dropped into the side but they still got a few of us. We opened up at the Germans; I was lying on my back firing a Tommy gun. Most of them had passed and they were away before you could say cat Robinson.

Then we moved into a holding position. We cleared a place for the armoured to get into. We just waited then for everybody to get in a line across the southern part of Italy. You could see that we were coming now to high ground, into the centre of Italy. The ports were held. There was plenty of demolition going on as the Germans must have realised that we were there in strength and they had to drop back.

One other thing was, that went back to the Volturno, and there were loads of bailey bridges that we had to bring forward. We built this bridge and then two of our engineering armoured vehicles; they carried what we called a scissors breech. We found that we got over this business there was steep banks which the tanks had trouble getting over. It was very soft ground. We went passed these and put these scissor bridges down so that armoured cars and Bren carriers could. We then got a few more of them to do and then up to where we cleared the areas up. We were now waiting for ammunition to come up and all the tanks were taking it and the carriers were taking it up and so on. Now we knew we were going on again.

There was on a high ground to the left there was a little Italian village. There seemed to be a wall on our side. What we were going to do was going to pincer but not climb to it, to get round left and right, which the Germans didn't know what has happening, and the Germans had heavily mined the area. So when we got split into two – sappers I am now talking about, mortar shells were now being slung over the top to stop any reinforcements coming forward. They did something as you could see smoke coming over. Then we attempted to come up the left, then we had very heavy machine gun fire at us, two of the lads got hit and two of the lads got killed. We then had to crawl forward and we found the mines. They were Italian Schuemines. Anyway provided you lifted the lid you could take the charge out. It was a flap on top, if you pushed the flap down it took the pin out and off it went.

When then went as far round as we could. We had a bit of tape on the back of Jimmy Hardman, and we pulled out which stake was safe ground. If you could call it safe ground! In any case now some of the infantry was coming up now, and they were following us. There was this sergeant with a Bren, he kept trying to get off this bloody path, and I said "you go off the path you might send something up!"

Anyway we got found and our section opened up what we had there, we were then innocent bystanders to all of this. We couldn't move as I had a mine detector wrapped round my neck. Eventually we got into the centre of this village. The infantry that was coming up now was following this tape. Once the Germans knew the tape was there they used a very small mortar and they had bazookas. I learnt about these bazookas later on. They went straight up into the air and straight down; they reckoned that they could drop a mine onto the back of an infantry man.

I never bothered to find out but they were a prize capture. Our infantry used to hang onto them; they used to fit on to our rifles that fired these hand grenades. They seem to part of the German rifle. Anyway eventually it took us two or three hours and they had to wait until we got to the other side of the village. Of course the Italians had taken shelter in some of the stronger houses of the village. Eventually we had Italians beckoning us on from the windows. We didn't know if they were doing it for us or for the Germans. We eventually took this whole village.

You could then see this road that went out; I forget where it leads to. Once our mortar officers got up there and our artillery up there. The church was still standing the Germans used to blow the tops of them. We had a marvellous view of all our tanks firing and everything else all going up in the air and onto this road. Our hurricanes and Boston Bombers – American, they came over.

There was a big concentration of transport just out of sight from us; we could see where the bombs were coming down. We could see the ack ack's opening up. They did it on purpose; all you had to do was keep away from them. We did hear German tanks, you can tell German from our tanks as their tanks are iron shod and ours did have rubber. You could hear the blasted tanks not see them. I always remembered an Australian soldier told us many moons ago he said "Mate if you want to stay alive, keep away from tanks". I don't know if he knew we were in an armoured brigade then.

The German was a very good fighter. When he stood and fought he fought. Suddenly they would just disappear and drop back as they did here. When we built up our reserves coming across from Palermo and Foggia, they suddenly just pulled back and they were now going past Naples and they left a very tragic bombing behind. They built a bomb into the main courtyard and it exploded and killed quite a few. I wasn't in Naples then as we were at the bottom of some mountain. I forget the name, but we could see the Rapido River. Although we never attempted to cross it the ones that did got a headache. We then went back to the Adriatic side and pushed onto, possibly the worst battles apart from Anzio that I ever took part in. we had comes across quite a few rivers but this was quite a brute – the Sangro River.

We then found out that we could carry on with our little episode. We were jumping over rivers like no ones business. Now every river as far as I was concerned was similar to a D-day. There were mine fields, sniping and pitch battles especially with the tanks.

Battle of Sangro

Unfortunately it was now coming into winter. There was rain and eventually snow. Before the snow came we moved up to the Sangro valley and the bridge – the longest in Europe had been blown up. The pillars were still standing there. This was something that happened. We went in well away from the Sangro, our brigade put all the sappers, and the infantry was coming up in Bren carriers and armoured cars in a sort of cutting, well away from the sea as that's where the Canadians were.

Getting off we moved off to the worst battle I have been in. The first assault the Indians went across with our armour. They were really tanked out. There was a fusilier battalion with them. When they stormed up this road there was terrific fire power came down – mortar fire, just at the end of the road there was three anti-tank guns and they played havoc with the trucks.

There were quite a few small rivers but nothing that compared to the Sangro. As I said before I never seen the four armoured coming through the cutting and as you got up top before you went down to the Sangro, you could look back and there was this great column of tanks, Bren carriers and whites cars as far back as you could see. There were engineers, infantry, and mortar men with mortars. As soon as we got to our break area we went to relieve the infantry division that was going to cover for the crossing of the Sangro. This took part some time afterwards I already told about the mill, the s mines and the patrols across the river.

The main assault was put off because of this rain, and when it rained it Italy It did rain! Nothing about sunny Italy or See Naples and die or some bloody thing as that!

We were stretched about over a couple of miles. When you sat on the tanks you could see the long line of tanks and armoured vehicles ready to go onto the Sangro. It was the first time I had seen the whole brigade strung out this road. We were going towards the Sangro River. As I said before we were specialists on river crossings. I don't know how. This was one of the worst crossings we had ever been in.

As they got onto the road behind the Sangro River and they split up and went to

201

different points ready for the assault. The assault was put off because of the rain. The rain made the river rise. Our first task when we got to the river was to build a bridge; this bridge was under water so it was hid. It was quite high banks. We put two bridges across. In the meantime we went mine clearing and finding the mine fields.

The bridge had been blown and it was the longest bridge in Italy I think at the time. *Bridges were often given a name, from the campaign: 'Sangro' Bridge, Construction dates: 4-14 December 1943. Details: 1,126ft long Class 30 Bridge, which spanned the river Sangro. It was the longest Bailey bridge built during the whole campaign.*

The Bailey bridge was certainly one of the major inventions of the War and one that has been even more successful in peacetime. It was a sectionalised construction, which was 'pinned' together and floated out over the river on a series of pontoons. Sir Donald Bailey designed the Bailey bridge in 1940, specifically to meet a requirement for a 40-ton capacity bridge. In July 1941 production of the Bailey bridge begun, by December 1941 the Bailey bridge was with the troops.

The production figures are staggering; a total of over 490,000 tons of Bailey bridge was manufactured, representing 200 miles (320 Km) of fixed bridges and 40 miles (64 Km) of floating bridges. Without doubt the bridge did much to shorten the course of the War, a view expressed by Montgomery who wrote in 1947: 'Bailey Bridging made an immense contribution towards ending World War II. As far as my own operations were concerned, with the Eighth Army in Italy and with the 21 Army Group in North West Europe, I could never have maintained the speed and tempo of forward movement without large supplies of Bailey Bridging'

The Engineers also had another tool, by which a bridge could be quickly provided, in the form of Bridge laying tanks. Several variants were deployed, but the development of a 30ft, 30-ton folding ("scissor") bridge began in 1936 for mounting on a tank. Initially due to the power and availability of the Covenanter, a number of MK I and MK II's were fitted with the production type scissor bridge, which was laid by hydraulic ram and arm installed in the fighting compartment and the power taken from the engine fan drive.

So we came up to the Sangro River. That was one of the worst, no it was the second worst rivers battle, the first and worst was Anzio. This one was really nasty, there was lifting mines and explosions and all the rest of it. Eventually we went up to the river and we made our HQ in a mill this side of the river, the British side. All the troops there were Canadian or British. The target was a place called Pescara, this was Mezzogiorno, and we could see the Germans walking about if you used the glasses.

The night we eventually made the crossing there was beaten back by the river, we arrived on the other side of the river wet through and we found five or six prisoners we found in a slit trench. A bit further up before we managed to knock out a SP gun that was up there, it wasn't firing where the bridge was, it was firing up the air. Every night we went across the river in single file. It was defined the best way up; we laid charges in the banks as they were pretty high. I doubt that any of our armour would get up. So what we had to do was use explosives and blow the banks down. We made sure they weren't watching when we did it and we never fired them until we certain day, so we covered them up and went back.

Sappers can be massed up quickly unlike tanks as we were in small sections. We were clearing mines and getting the bridge ready. The Germans were well dug in on the other side, we couldn't get up the bank we had to wait for artillery and mortars to get us a boost and get their heads down. We did see an edge of some sort and we thought once we got to that we would be safe. We did have Bren guns and Tommy guns, in any case we knew in a few minutes the infantry would be coming across. I think they were mechanised infantry of the 7th Armoured. The tanks were going into position and most of them were beginning to fire. Anyway we got onto this edge and it was quite a sort of deep edge.

We could hear the bullets coming over the top and the shells coming from our side. Anyway in about three or four hours we moved forward and we were taking prisoners. We started taking quite a lot of prisoners and the German side stops firing. We then got into the place where the Germans were and there was a few still in there. We made sure that their weapons were away, and we waited for tanks to come up and we were away. The mines were cleared and we were now pushing onto the new objective. Their objective was different to ours we were there under sufferance.

I am going to describe some of the technical horrors of war. Sapper work is pretty deadly anyway and we had to drag out mines. When we went across the Sangro river I was with the 626-field squadron 4th armoured brigade, we lifted mines to get the tanks across and when we were on the second day of the assault, the infantry had taken a terrible bashing on the road from the Sangro river bridge which we had blown to Mezzogiorno, which was the main village in the hills just above, it was about 2 ½ to 3 miles long literally in scores.

The other jobs we done, the Germans laid s-mines, these are the ones that jump up in the air, and they laid them in circles. In fact in some there were 16 to 18 mines in a circle. Once they put them all in the sapper –

the German sapper, he used to take out the little pin that held these in. They used to cover them over, in time the ground would grow back, and you couldn't tell the difference. On some of them you couldn't see the prongs.

How we found them we had to use a detector. We found them, stuck the bayonet in and we went round the circle, and found how many were there. How we disarmed we had to screw them off, we had to make sure that hadn't put igniters and you couldn't find them. We used to cut pins from the wire to poke through to stop the thing coming down and striking it. It if fired it jumped in the air, if one went up, the lot went up. You had to time it of course.

Eventually we done this circle and a fellow would come from the next circle, and he said "he had to run out of blinking wire" so we had to go and help him. They had done half of them. As I said we worked in threes. We then cleared it and went to the side. There was schuemines to the side, they were easy to find but best left alone. If the top part comes out then it pushed the pin out and bobs your uncle. There was a voice, and

I thought blimey they have found us but it was American.

Jeep said "Throw a grenade and run like hell", I said "Well it could be someone, remember all these prisoners had been loosened by the Italians", and he said "yeah, but why take a chance". So I said "listen", and we heard it again "American soldiers?" I thought bloody hell, eventually it was a boy about 12 years old. It would appear that his father was an American and he had come home on leave and the Italian army had grabbed him, and conscripted him, as he was Italian.

His two boys who were over there had been born in America with American passports, but they didn't recognise the passport of the father. They said "Are you coming back with us?" and they said "no, my grandmother, and grandfather are over here". I said "we are British", and he said "No we have a lot of British", "what do you mean?", and he said "We have British, American, Yugoslav soldiers", I said "where?" "They are hiding under the mill and the Germans are in the Garden". I said "Bloody hell, I will make you go and see them and then tell them the British is nearly here, but for Christ's sake go very carefully". "I know this" he said "I have seen them putting the mines in". "Oh" I said "Where are they?"

He showed us them down by the river, and he walks along a safe area. There is a house down by the river where he goes in and smokes. He then said "there is a path down there and it is not mined". We come up to two haystacks on the side and the Germans are underneath the haystacks. We go back to the mill and the nipper went to his mill. We went across to our mill, we then went and saw our officers and they went to the Intelligence Officer of the Royal Fusiliers, and he said "Are you sure there are British troops over there, its not a trap at all?" and I said "no he sounded quite reasonable and sensible for a nipper". "Right" he said "we have to alter our artillery fire now because of this house". There was another big house up further where all the Italians had gone into hide.

Now this is what happened. Two days afterwards we decided to go across the river and get these men out. I was going to go across as I knew where the schue mines were, but what that nipper had told us about the house and where the sentry was. So we brought a section of the 4th Indian Infantry division. I think they were called the Rajpour Rifles, and the officers said "If there is a sentry there God help him". These fellows got across, I think they were Pathans. I saw them and they had knives I reckon these knives were as long as our bayonets. I think they preferred them over our bayonets. I thought hope they bloody know my uniform and I am not a German.

We went across the river and sure enough there was the house. There was another funny thing about the house, we could see the front door, and it had some sand bags at the side. One of the Pathans went in and there was no one in there, but there were voices down below. After we had done our dirty work we had got these out – they were Italians. All the women and children came out. They got the sentry I don't think they killed him. They wanted to see what he was.

The ones who were underneath this straw or haystack, two Pathans just slung in two grenades and out some of them came but not just yet. We went into the mill with this Intelligence Officer and there was two kids waiting. They called down and moved bundles of chestnuts. Down below there were American, British, Polish, and Yugoslavs. So the officer said "Single file", you never smelt anything like it in all your life. As they were coming out he told the mill owner and his wife to get packed and come with them, as they might get prizes over what they had done. We got them back to the river and in single file they all went across. Then our Intelligence officer had a go through all the POW's. One lad was a Hampshire and he got taken away. He told me things about Pompey that I didn't know. Anyway off they went and then the following day in went the attack. Unfortunately by this time the Jerry mortars were playing about and unfortunately at this time too there was an Indian transport company with mules in the courtyard and about three or four bombs dropped about them, and I saw some terrible sights in there. The Muleteers were actually crying over their mules, they were shooting them after the bombardment had finished.

I did meet a lot of members of the old Hampshire Heavy Regiment which I was in when I was a territorial. They were Prisoners that were taken at Tibore, the batteries and the infantry that I was in – the Hampshire regiment. In most cases they had been hid by the Italians. We found quite a lot later on especially when we got up to the Sangro River.

All our ex-prisoners were taken back for interrogation and we now prepare for the assault on the top village which was called Mezzogiorno. I still get nightmares over this.

We went across the river on the tanks, we got across quite easily as some of our troop had blown gaps in the bank. As we went up to Mezzogiorno the most concentrated fire that I had ever been in came down on us. The infantry was the Punjabis, they got terrible casualties and tanks were rolled over. My mate from our section was crouching down by the side of a tank when it hit him and I think half the blinking track went through his stomach. The Punjabis didn't half take a big wallop there. We got up towards Mezzogiorno and the Germans were coming from everywhere, they were throwing grenades at our tanks and we had to drop back, right to the river. We had mortars on the other side – a London regiment. They opened up and pushed the Germans right back past this village of Mezzogiorno. A lot of our tanks were ok, and there weren't grenades, we had a lot of anti tank rockets.

They used to keep quiet and when our tanks got past them, they kept quiet and when our tanks retreated they opened up. We managed on the second attack to get into another mill the Mezzogiorno Mill. In there was some of Ghurkhas. They had been in there for a couple of weeks on and off, on our trips up and down. Another thing I will say our Grave Recognition Unit did a marvellous job, they were whipping the dead away. On the second or third attempt we went out to see that the Germans had put mines under our dead. We had to clear everything.

There were quite a few more rivers from the Volturno to the Sangro. Most of them were small, but it didn't matter how small the river, it was always dangerous to cross. We had the odd sniper and we did lose

213

a lot of men. I haven't explained much about losing men apart from that time when we were on the tanks and the mortar fire came across and killed quite a few of our lads.

I had my blinking arguments and I suppose I was on the hit list of a gentleman we used to call the "Medal Hunter" 626-field squadron this was, 4th Armoured Brigade. Anyway a couple of times I was on charges for conduct prejudious to good order and military discipline but this one was more serious.

We were going toward Echelon for the Sangro River crossing and this was one of my final clashes with authority, we were on the tanks going up to the Echelon and in front of us was a tank with some of our men on. One of our more senior officers said that it would look more military if we got on to the tank which is what we did.

There were about 12 of us on one tank; we were huddled together as the tank was close to going below the level of this cutting we were going through. As I looked back I could see the whole brigade in a long line of tanks, armoured cars, and ones with tracks. We couldn't get off, but I think we shouldn't have been on them, as this is what happened.

Our squadron of engineers went in on the tanks. Their sappers had taken mines out before their advance, but during the night the German sappers had come and put the mines back and they had covered them up with the bodies of our dead. So when we went in we had 6 tanks, we had 3 tank corps and three 3 London yeomanry and they were Sherman's.

Mortar bombs were dropped on them.

The tank in front of ours was hit by spasmodic artillery fire from the Germans, and the whole lot (seven men) were killed, and it was listed as we found out later, as six men killed, and one man missing. They said according to the minutes of the war diary, that they were sheltering, they were not they were on top of the bloody tank. We couldn't get off as were in a cutting on the way down to the river. We came to the river and we put up bridges, and to try and keep dry.

One of the tanks had 16 of the men around, and first of all it was given out that 5 were killed, 10 were wounded and one was missing. Well three or four days later we went back and the Germans just lobbing some shells all over the place. We were going out to our echelons and they had hit this tank and that was that happened.

On the 6th November 1943 the following men gave their lives from 626 field squadron: -

- *Fish, Stanley James, age: 24, service no: 2073051. Son of Mr and Mrs. Albert fish, of Small Dole, Sussex.*
- *Bryceland, Thomas, age: 27, service no: 2012360.*
- *Darlington, William Thomas, age: 32, service no: 2152333. Son of Fredrick and Laura Ann Darlington; husband of ivy Darlington, of st. Austell, Cornwall.*
- *Dawtry, Ronald, age: 24, service no: 2079041.*

The men that lost their lives on the 29th November 1943 and are buried at Sangro River War Cemetery, from 626 field squadron are as follows: -

- *Smart, John Gilbert, age: 26, service no: 2117303. Son of George and Annie smart; husband of Minnie smart, of Otley, Yorkshire.*
- *Statham, Leslie Frederick, driver, age: 23, service no: 14529552. Son of Frederick and Laura Emma Statham, of Tamworth, Staffordshire; husband of Alice Statham, of Tamworth.*
- *Raffan, James Smith, age: 23, service no: 2075082. Son of James and Margaret W. Raffan, of Woodside, Aberdeen.*
- *Priestly, Cyril, age: 29, service no: 2135921. Son of Joseph and Kathleen Priestley, of Barnsley, Yorkshire; husband of Eva Priestley, of Barnsley.*
- *Jones, John, age: 22, service no: 5124852. Son of Thomas and Nancy Jones, of St. Helens, Lancashire.*

We now had to leave the wounded, and when we got to the river. We could see the river but not the tanks as they weren't there. They were all going into echelons and camouflage ourselves before we crossed the river.

We got into Echelon, and got ready to go across the river, and unfortunately it started to rain, so it was put off, put off again, and put off again, meanwhile we went back to make that the men that were killed, when we were coming up the river were in a safe position for the grave recognition unit, we had been told that on the minutes by our company sergeant major that one was missing and that he could have been anywhere, could have deserted.

We were now going across after the battle and I had words about the conduct of putting all our sections on tanks as we were going towards the start line of the Sangro River. According to some of the minutes I have got of the 626-field squadron unit and this applied on our way to the Sangro, the big battle there. 6 men killed one man missing they said according to the minutes of the war diary that they were sheltering, they were not they were on top of the bloody tank. Of course jerry was ranging up and down and anyway a shell landed on top of the tank, they weren't hiding and as it said in the minutes and in this case they were all killed.

When we got there, we found the men where we left them, put them in, groundsheets and left them for the grave recognition unit which came up while we were there, we then looked around to try to find the man that was missing, we first found his gas mask which had his ID we then started looking for the ID that was round his neck, which we found eventually and told our sergeant major that we had found it and bits and pieces that we picked up we put in the gas mask case together with the two ID tags. Anyway the grave recognition unit said that was enough for to find out the bits and pieces that was a terrible thing to muck about with, we went back right across Italy to Cassino.

From the Unit Diary 29ᵗʰ November 1943

04:15 Troops left on three tanks

14:30 1 troop: 6̶ 7 killed, 10 wounded, 1̶ ̶m̶i̶s̶s̶i̶n̶g̶ through one shell which burst a tank. (Crossing out as was found in the diary thanks to Fred's efforts)

The company sergeant major said that he would now talk to the company clerk, who made out the war diary and change it. We had a lot of argument with our senior officers (the junior officers were alright) we then went back and down to a mill, which was on the river, and prepared for the crossing, we went backward and forward lifting mines before the battle started. When the battle started we moved down to the river, dug in, and put explosives into the side of the river so that when the assault went in, we could make a ramp so that our armour could get up the banks because the bridge had been blown, and it was the longest bridge in Italy at the time. When the attack started, we first of all tried to get to the village of Mezzigronia, and we suffered appalling losses especially with the 4ᵗʰ infantry division.

Eventually we had to come back, very nearly to the edge of the river on the German side, and dig in. Meanwhile the Germans had come back to pick up the dead, and had laid mines and covered the mines with our dead. We then attacked after removing our dead, and the mines, and we lost three tanks in the first assault (but only tracks off) which could be fixed, so the gunners and tank crews stayed in their tanks, and supplied artillery fire, and machine gun fire, when required. They were just out of range of some anti tank guns (which we found out later were laid up on the road) there were three of them, but once we got forward and go into another big mill, we could see the German gunners and when we opened up, they had to pull back. This allowed our tanks which had been recovered and the tracks replaced, to come up and take their place, and we got from Mezzigronia, into or on the way to a railway station, we then had to stop and two British divisions and a Canadian division took over and went forward.

The Germans knew we were coming they slung everything into the river, and it was raining. We taken the path to

Mezzigronia, our sappers and their sappers were clearing the mines as fast as we had cleared them. We could only get them out and onto the side, as men were dropping dead. Eventually we did get to the top but under great stress and there was this second mill. Some of men were hiding in there. All our sappers of what were left of them, we regrouped along with the Royal Fusiliers, they were having a go at the front of the house and a sniper was firing into the mill.

We now went into the real battle stations to get in. Our sergeant, who was the only NCO, went doolally; mind you he was getting on a bit. He went into the mill and that was his lot. He wouldn't come out, and eventually he was taken away. We went up to the river with the Royal Fusiliers, and they wanted us to take over and make up their numbers. We were getting the tanks sorted out. A corporal got wounded and we had no NCO. We just did our own thing. Of course three of our sappers had just gone the youngest one had been hit, when one of the tanks had gone on a mine and the track had gone up and hit him. I don't know what happened to him, he was taken away.

We then went into the mill, down the bottom of the mill. We were going to sweep to a mill, just below Mezzogiorno. What we didn't know was that all the Italians from Mezzogiorno had taken refuge in the bottom of the mill. Unfortunately quite a large family had come down from Mezzogiorno, down towards the Sangro river and they had set of s-mines and the whole lot of them women, children, babies and the old fellow that was leading them were all killed, and they were at the side of the road.

We then got ready for the assault. We found some Indians in the church from the first assault. There was some Ghurkhas. The Royal Fusiliers went up the road. There was this memorial in the middle of this square and one of the lads fired a Piet mortar at this tank and it hit and blew it up, as it was full of this petrol it was firing. Soon as they started jumping out of the tanks the Ghurkhas came running out of this church, and one of the Germans were caught but he was dead. He must have been stretched about 8 or 9 feet bits of him everywhere. Everything settled down, but the fusiliers went straight into a schmizzer. I thought he was dead but he wasn't. Most of the tanks were coming up.

Our first night in the shelter, we were out of NCOs', myself and Jeep went forward after the sergeant of the Fusiliers said "Someone was putting a bullet through the mill". We took a Bren gun, when we saw the fire and the flash, we opened up with a Bren gun, and that quietened him down for a little bit. We could see before it got dark that there was mine on the road.

They came over to where we were and they said, "what's happening?" and we told them that there was an assault going in but this had petered out by now and that we would have to stay here until we got communication through for our brigade – this was the 4th Armoured brigade. That wasn't very long. Up comes our sergeant and with another wireless as our wireless had packed up. He told us we were going to hang on for a day and then the following day we were going to assault again, and he wanted to know how many men was there. Fresh tanks had now got across the river as the river had dropped – this was in a period of heavy rainfall.

What we didn't know that some of the Ghurkhas had got into a church on the side and the Royal Fusiliers had infiltrated the side one. We had no Armour, we had to go back and check on our armour, and we had eight tanks coming up our road. At least half them had their tracks knocked off exploded on mines.

To make matters worse a lot of the men who died on the road were covering the mines. So before we had to get to the mines we had to remove the dead. Some of the tanks had run over some of the men. It made it a very blasted business. Anyway we got some of the men who were dead to the side of the road and we had cleared some of the mines from the road. They were mostly teller mines which were easy to clear. Then we got them to the side of the road and we had to warn tanks not to touch them and keep away at least three or four from the side of the road. Of course we had the dead men were on the side.

After we got one tank up to the head of the road, then we found out something else. Two of the Indians who were left and went off a recce and had found that there was a battery of German anti-tank guns; they couldn't see where we were now but they could see the beginning when we come onto the road. There were three of them together which was wasteful I thought.

Now our horror started we had to squirm around on our knees so they couldn't see us and we had to sort of roll our dead off mines and into the verge to get the mines out so we could get our tanks up. We had got about half way up the road doing this unpleasant job when the first tank came out from this escarpment. Of course three German anti tanks guns spotted us and they opened up, and the tank that was avoiding that was run off that road and was buried. Up the road was six of tanks but the stench from the dead was terrible. The next day we went across again, the Germans had come back and put the mines back. Unfortunately some of the lads that were killed went across the mines.

The next tank that came out but his bloody tracks came off but his gun was all right. We had to then go back and sweep around it. So that the next tank out could go past it and onto Mezzogiorno road. By this time we had got as close up to the mill and we could see the flashes from where the anti tank gun was coming. And our wireless OP radioed back the exact position where these anti tank guns were and we had a very good regiment of 25 pounders and they certainly put them into action. Although they didn't destroy the guns they did destroy the crews. The next three tanks out go out as far as we were but they couldn't get round the corner. There was another anti tank regiment – German – up further in about the centre of Mezzogiorno.

Anyway we collected enough Royal Fusiliers and Indian division; eventually they quietened these guns down. The tank backed into and then used shellfire to destroy the guns. By the then they had run off. Every so often all the tanks that were knocked out used to fire just one shot to let everyone know we were still there. The tank drivers were repairing them on the road. There was one that wasn't on a mine but it was on the edge of the mine, so we had to get under the tank and dig it out. We passed it out through the escape hatch, as we didn't know if we were being observed. There is an escape hatch right underneath a Sherman's tank. The mine was passed by, as there were two tanks together as we had to go under one to get to the other one. The tank drivers had got half the ones knocked out, they had got two back on the road by the morning.

Then the next attack went in. We were told more infantry would be joining the Royal Fusiliers. We got out of the road and we cleared the road, as they went round the corner. The leading fusiliers he got hit with a burst of schmizzer and down he went. They got him and dragged him back.

We heard one coming and it was a flame thrower. Of course when it come up to where the Ghurkhas were they opened up. He of course he turned round and then he started using his flame thrower at them. He was sticking on the wall and burning. The Fusiliers were the first ones in Italy to knock out a tank with a Piet Mortar; I have never seen anything like this. A piet mortar went forward and he fired it at the tank.

He hit it and there was a bloody big bang and it stopped. Before those tankies came out the Ghurkhas had come out that church and they were into these men, and they got them down. We then found – we had done a couple of excursions out but we knew that was a German tank out there but it turned out to be a flamethrower. A German tank had iron tracks so you could hear it but ours were mostly rubber tracks. You could hear them but you couldn't distinguish them. It was keeping its eye on this road, we had to get up. Now there was only one other way through and we had to blow our way through the houses using a piet mortar, which we hadn't used before. So anyway we got on up there and made some holes and made them a bit bigger.

      One of their officers had gone out with a placard and put on it "This tank was knocked out by Royal Fusiliers (what ever battalion it was), the first one to be knocked out by a Piet Mortar" we thought it was a wotsname. We lost far more men going up this road as at the far end of the road, there were only a few Germans but they had a spander, and they were sweeping the road. We were hanging around waiting for one of our tanks to come up. I think it was the City of London Yeomanry up he came and as soon as they put a couple of shells into where we thought this German machine gun was it was stopped dead and we were away.

We went back on our side and we were as lousy as coots. I have never seen lice as big as we had. We reported it and they said "Right as soon as the battle is finished we will send you and you will get deloused." Well we were itching and scratching. Every time we went to sleep we used to have to go bed in an Italian farmhouse. There were 8 of us in this bed all scratching and itching away.

My officer he was a git. This was just before we pushed out we went to our started station and we put on our clothes, Two pairs of socks on, and socks around my neck. The vest it was walking and jumping around with all these lice. A bit further down the officers were in their dug out and one of the lads, I shan't say who, found this git of an officer and he put his vest on the side of his bed so he got as lousy as we did. The other two officers were top right men. One of them was the son of a RM officer who was one of my bosses when I worked in the dockyard. How I found out as I said before I had a piece in my pay book that as I was a civil servant working in the dockyard and I was getting my money made up, as I joined up before the

Munich Crisis. They were not to pay me any money until the paymaster had been informed.

The next thing was we went towards the outside, and another column of tanks was coming up further to our left and the left of Mezzigronia. As they went across the field shell fire hit them and they went up the air as no ones business. The tanks were coming up past this square and there was a sign saying Pescara. The first tank was hit by anti tank fire, and the next one tried to push it to get the men up to safety. Then all the tanks started coming, the carriers full of KR's. They moved onto the main road and then silence. The Germans had gone. They had walked to Pescara.

They did say that the Germans called our tanks the Tommy cookers if they caught them they certainly knocked the seven names of wotsit out of them. In any case some of the got out and some didn't. We went into Mezzigronia. We through an orchard and made sure it was clear, we sheltered as there was small arms coming through and mortars going over head back to the river. Eventually it stopped and the armoured division on our right, which I think was Canadian. They got through and there was a race to Pescara.

Straight up then to Mezzigronia, at the same time we had to move the dead at the side of the road to look at the mines. Of course some of the mines that the Indians had slung out were still armed at the side of the road from the first assault. Anyway we did manage to get to the end of the road and into the village. Then there were snipers. We got our Bren gun lined up at them and soon as they flashed we let go with our Bren guns. We did have a PIAT (Projector, Infantry, Anti-Tank) mortar which no one seemed to know what it did but we soon found out.

Well we went forward out of the village and on to this track. Now of course all the tanks were coming up, unfortunately there was quite a few getting blown up. Not with mines but with gun fire, they were shelling them. We got into a ditch and we stayed there. The worst thing was and I remember this about keeping away from armour. The tank drew up right above us, a tankie officer shouted out" Are you getting fired at?" I thought bloody hell for Christ sake move! Anyway he took off when we told him we were alright. We just laid there when everything had died down all the funny noises and whistles stopped we went towards the place where we to make echelon. We cleared out waiting for our whites car came up with our gear and then we had some grub.

Now we went on until we found we were on top of this ridge and everything stopped. Then all the lads and trucks come up and we went on into some of these houses that were empty. We started to get ready for some food.

Then this medal hunter came up and he wanted our section forward again. Of course we were all eating then; the old man came out and said we don't want anymore. He said "We have got stay here now until we are sent for by the divisional CRE. " So thank Christ for that we had our grub and got our heads down.

At night time we had to stand to. We had these jerry cans we were going to fill with water but when we got back we told to prepare a water point. What we used to do was two big round canvas swimming pools was the only way I could describe them and we got near where this water was. Where this pump was pumping drawn up into these canvas things into a compound and stirred it all up. You could then pump it off into jerry cans.

Of course our brigade and all the tanks were coming up for water not only for drinking but for the engines as well. The Canadians used to come across and we would do a bit of bartering we would give them water and we wanted wine, and we would swap over. We used to have one jerry can of water for one jerry can of vino. We had two of these tanks going and when we were going, everyone came with jerry cans.

There was an ambulance and I am not sure what they were Friends of the earth or something? They were mostly people who didn't like fighting and they were American, there ambulances were all over the place. We had three or four following us, very soul destroying when you see those ambulances. Anyway we were very glad of them later on. That was not in the 4th Armoured Brigade but in the 1st Infantry division, 24th Guards Brigade.

We had to then go out into the open, which was on top of the hill and then slightly down towards Pescara. We were now on top and we could look down on the Germans and we could see the Germans were scarpring and they were pulling out. They did, they went back as far as Pescara, and we followed them back to Pescara and we fired up there for two or three days until all the divisions came up there, because of all the ships that were lost at Bari, the winter offensive was stopping so we were told to dig in. So that's what we did.

We done our little bit and then there was this nasty little bush telegraph again that we were going to go over to Casino. As we started to go down to Pescara the Germans disappeared again, then they popped up on the other side of Pescara. As we went in. now a Canadian division took over and now we were supporting them. By the time we had worked our way into Pescara we realised that we couldn't go any further. Anyway there was a bit of rumpus at Pescara; we blew all these drinks up as the drinking was getting out of hand. All the kits went onto the Lorries, white's cars and Bren carriers, and there was blinking great convoy went right across this valley. We followed the

Sangro River for a lot of the way and came in just below Casino, the monastery. We pulled back and laboured up. Then something nasty happened, apart from getting sent out from 626 field squadron.

Our old troop went across the Rapido River. We more or less then knew that when they assaulted Casino proper, the American and the French were going up the Casino gap with the Mediterranean. The Brits were going up lake the Rapido River and on the previous crossing the Americans got slaughtered. They really got slaughtered. We had a couple of the sergeants from the company that tried to get across there and they said "you have our sympathies when you start this lot". Fortunately we didn't go that way.

Bari

This was my experience when we went down to Bari to get deloused. It had been in and out of Italian Farms; sleeping in barns we were as lousy as coots. A troop of RE's from the 6th Armoured Brigade and two troops from the Canadian Armoured Brigade which we were attached to, were down to Bari on December 1st. We went down by trucks and they dropped us off at the big hospital that they had. Alongside that was a delousing centre, where we put all our clothes into the fire and got them de-loused. The Italians washed our underclothes, so for the time being all we had was our battle dresses and overcoats, and blankets. They didn't have to wash those, so we put them on and the only thing we were allowed to buy was a pair of socks as we were wearing our boots. When you go to get deloused, you just get your hair cut, spread with DT – after a shower of course and then the clothes get baked. Then you should be alright which we were.

So we then went to our places for sleeping, which was in an Italian house they had taken over. The only thing we were missing then was food. The Canadians came up with their grub and said you could have some of this. Well we messed with them. When we got our clothes back from the wash, what they used to do was wash them, and hang them up in a big barn (not outside as they would have froze) to dry them out. When we got them we put them on, and we were more or less a bit warmer.

Then that night, it was about the 2nd of December, one German Reconnaissance plane came over and noticed the ships in Bari harbour. There were about 17 including oil tankers and ammunition boats. The Italian harbours are like two pincers with just a small opening for the ships to come through. Once they hit a tanker, all the oil went everywhere. Before you could say Jack Robertson there were about 100 or 200 German aircraft coming over. They knew how to exploit anything. All they did was strafed, and bombed. The Canadian officer in charge of the Canadians grabbed our sergeant and we were getting all our kit together as when some of the ships were exploding shells and bombs and god knows what went up in the air, and they came down all around us. So we legged it up the road as fast as could with our kit.

Eventually we came to this farm and we went into this barn. Then we watched it was like Guy Fawkes Night. It was flares, and bombs and god know what. These aircraft kept coming in, they didn't seem to bother with the town but certainly knocked seven kinds of wotsit our of Bari harbour. It put back the advance of the 8th Army; we then slowed up at a place called Pescara when we did get back to our unit.

There was a huge cloud of smoke and flames which came up the road to where we were. There were a lot of sailors coming into our place and they said it was mustard gas that was on some of the boats. I don't know if it was true, but we were trying to keep away from the smoke. Anyway the following day a lot of Canadian trucks came up and we went with them, and took us back to our unit which was then 626 field squadron, and I don't know if anyone else went down there but that was the end of our escapade.

What the Germans had done by accident, that the Liberty Ships, which were carrying ammunition for winter offensives against the Germans, were all caught in Bari. An oil tanker had been hit and so had about 17 other ships, some carrying ammunition and they all went. Of course this is what we needed now!

After this episode at Bari we got up and rejoined our unit. We got back up as far as Pescara and because of all the ammunition and oil that had been lost at Bari, which we all knew about. The offensive was called off. Pescara became our front line base. There was a very glorious place as far as we were concerned. One day we were checking some of the houses for booby traps. The Canadians came over and said Oi, there is a wine distillery just up there, and will you check it in case there are any booby traps in it. I said yeah, we walked over and had a look at it.

It appeared it had been used by the Germans as a sort of dressing station – medical dressing station. So we checked it and it was all right, so the Canadians said alright lets have a look and see what's around. Down below there were these huge casks upright, they were full of vino. So anyway we went back and got every jerry can we could find and as our billet was well spread out – no one saw us actually. Anyway we got these jerry cans and washed them out and we filled them up with this vino. I think that this one of the reasons about why we sang "have we a friend like old Joe Stalin" which went down very well with some of our senior officers. Anyway we got back to our unit we had a special dug out for it and we went back on our mine clearing episodes. The Canadians were enjoying themselves.

Unfortunately the top of the cask was open. Someone must of got drunk and fell in. Don't know who it was whether it was one of ours or theirs. It could have been one of the Germans left behind. Anyway at about an hour, up come red caps and they riddled these drums and there was vino up to their knees in this cellar, before it drained away.

Maggie May

So we knew it was kaput with the supply ships being hit. We were going to stay there for the winter until our supplies came over. The Maggie May Tavern started in Africa and I was in the 4th Armoured Brigade. How we turned this, was the unit painter, painted Maggie May tavern. We used to put two whites cars 6 feet apart, and tarpaulin across the top. This was at night time so we could have a light. Wine that had been liberated or swapped was passed round in mugs. Maggie May Tavern name came from our cook who was a Liverpudlian. Maggie May song was the anthem of Liverpool. It went through Africa, Sicily and Italy. It was still going strong.

We used to after engagement check out how many boots we had got to fill the drink for the troop, what we used to do many of the lads that were unfortunately killed, use their boots. This was the number one currency, instead of slinging them, we used to get a jeep and go round the farms "Vino for scarpa". That may sound callous but that was that. In one episode I got half a sheep, or a little pig or bloody great jugs of vino.

We used to use to use our biscuit tins for our hard tack. When we used to get it back, we had two very good young officers they used to give us their spirits as they didn't drink.

All the vino was poured into these big biscuit tins we got and we used to sit in circles and talk about home and what ever it was. We passed this around and sing, and we would always end on the same song, our senior officer didn't go much on, the officers didn't join in. Russia was doing very well and so the song was "Have we a friend like Old Joe Stalin".

We used to pour that into to it, to give it a bit of body. Then we sit round in the circle, and we only had one mug. We then passed it round. That was our drinking spasms. We used to always finish and this would get up the nose of some of the senior officers, a song – "Have we a friend like old Joe Stalin, no not one, no not one. Old Joe knows all about our troubles, he will fight until the war is won. Have we a friend like old Joe Stalin. No not one, no not one." Or the Maggie May one and I spoke about our little episode on the way to Algiers on our third trip.

We were singing our hearts out and up came the song "Have we a friend like old Joe Stalin" about 5 seconds later one of the officers came over and said "Oi the old man said shut up". So discretion is the best part of valour and we all shut up and went back to sleep.

The song that we used to sing even in Africa as well Italy was "Have we a friend like Old Joe Stalin" because the Russians were doing very well, urging us to open a second front. Churchill said it was the soft underbelly of the Axis. Some axis and some belly! Anyway "Have we a friend like old Joe Stalin", it took off very well with the British troops. A lot of the officers never liked it, they considered it unpatriotic. Then again we used to sing it and that was that. That was the song that sent me off to Anzio.

Little Porky Pig - Italy

On our left was a very big Italian farm. In some sties they had a few pigs. Overnight we used to get talking with the New Zealanders, as we used to get some drink, as I said before we used to change our boots for vino. We were all sitting around talking. There was a big Maori who was their butcher.

He said "There is a pig in one of them sties, but unfortunately there is a watch on this sty by the Italians." So one night the New Zealanders and some of our fellows too, they got some of the signal grenades to make a noise. Now if even mortar or shell fire came over the Italians used to go the dugout at the back of their farm. So they got all their family out, who was guarding the pig and whipped it out. They got it all down into this dugout they had dug, as soon as they got out of sight. I think there were 5 lads – two of ours and three of theirs.

Before the poor pig knew what had happened he had his throat slit. He was put on a stretcher and carried out. Of course the Italians had thought it had run away. As they had left the door open but there was blood all over the place. We went down to this river about a mile away. They got a big oil drum; we used cordex to blow the end off. Charcoal was one of the main things that the Italians used, and not far from us, was a big fascine dump and huge heap of charcoal.

We got a few bags of this charcoal including some fascines of sticks. Took them up, cleaned the pig, shaved the pig – all the hair off, and then bunged him into the oil drum which was clean. We then sealed it and built the fire with charcoal all around the drum apart from the top part. Then we left it, there a bit of glow but no flames. In the morning, this Maori went down and carved this pig up that had been well cooked now. He handed it out. Now company, our cooks anyway were renowned at making bread. They supplied the bread and the New Zealanders supplied the bacon. It was a very very good feed; I shall always remember that pork. We left a load of corn dog and corn beef for him to sort of square him up a bit I think and soap which they were short of.

Another thing on mind now, we were experts on crossing rivers, coming across fro Taranto up to the Sangro. There must of have been a dozen, the worst ones I have said were the Trigno and the Sangro. Now the 8th Army was moving across Italy and moving towards Naples. They were in front eventually after two or three days and various stops we got to Naples and then went to Cassino. Cassino there was a river, and the Americans got really really murdered there and it was called the Rapido. I couldn't see any of our people could overtake Cassino unless they crossed the Rapido and went up the valley that was along side that was heading towards Rome. We never bothered to see that, we had a look round the Rapido, it was a massive river. Compared to Sangro it was a stream. We went back to near Cassino.

Cassino

From Pescara, we went round to Cassino and from Cassino we went to Anzio. When we were sorted out as very good sappers, that's the ones they wanted to get shot of. Right in front of my tent as I opened it was Cassino Monastery. I was placed under arrest, no one told anything about it. The next morning I shaved and appeared before the old man, I think his name was Smith, he was a pretty tense person as far as I was concerned, the second in command was the one I didn't go much on and it was this. The Company Sergeant Majors name was Croucher and he came from Aldershot and he was a decent fellow. The second in command wasn't, he was the one I was arguing with about the man that was blown to pieces and he said was missing. He wasn't missing he was dead. If he was listed as missing his family wouldn't get any money. He said he would now talk to the Company Clerk who made out the war diary and change it. Anyway we had a lot of arguments with our senior officers, the junior officers was all right. Anyway I got weighed off come up conduct prejudice to good order and military discipline and that was my card towards Anzio.

A few days afterwards we were alerted to go to across country and that was to Cassino where we had a few ups and downs, and I finished up with 40 day Royal Warrant. I thumped the bloody corporal who kept getting on my nerves. Anyway just after the fracas my name was the first one out, the lads were ready to go to Anzio and we were to join the 23rd Field Company. Of course the old man came down and said they wanted the best of the best. We all knew that the "Have we a friend like old Joe Stalin" and my 40 day warrant figured in this somehow. 40 day warrant meant you didn't go to the nick. No use going to the nick in a place like that. Everyday you were going to get killed or thought you were going to get killed. I didn't!

Before Anzio

This is just before we went to Anzio; we had come after the week in Pescara we had come right across Italy to Naples and from Naples we went up to Cassino. We had a reputation of being top notch for bridging and getting across the rivers. In fact I have got a photograph of all of us on a train in Dendi we used to be called the rope boys. There were 6 of us in a dinghy and we all carried ropes, and we used to get right across. We used to jump in them paddle like mad and we hear all the noises going on. We went down to Rapido and we had a nasty time trying to get across but to take Cassino you had to take Rapido first. There was another hill on the side, when we did go the French had to go first and also the Americans, Brits and the Poles went up as well, but the British had to take Mount Cassino, not Mount Cassino – Mount Kiro, and the poles had the tough job of taking Cassino itself and of course this was after they bombed it, and of course they should have done it earlier, it would saved a lot of lives.

Then we the distraction that half the sappers from the 7th Armoured Division were going to go somewhere else. We all thought that we going to invade the south of France, although we never had any idea until this happened. We became a re-enforcement regiment and there were sappers coming from other regiments as well. Infantry was getting made up on the spot, but we were going to go, as we may have been needed at the beginning of the advance wherever that was. We knew we weren't going to go home now. The code word was shingle, which put the kybosh on it. The next thing was loads of whites cars and we said goodbye to our mates we left behind. I think most of them went home and off we toddled. Again we thought about this mutiny at Salerno. The 8th Army came out of the hospital and instead of going back to their units and going home; they went into or told to go other units. They sat on their bags and didn't go anywhere, and I think three of the sergeants were sentenced to death. None of this appeared on orders; all this became lavatory gen or bushfire gen which ever you want to think about.

Anzio

We then moved across, tanks were finding it pretty hard. It was open country with hills and so when we got back to Cassino, and into Cassino. We had a little dabble at Cassino to let them know we were there. We then had to bridge up the Garieglearne River. We then went back into and we could see Cassino back on top of the hill.

We suddenly woke up, the whole troop, the whole brigade, moved up to the other side. We wondered what was wrong, as when we moved something was going to happen. We went through the mountains and I think the Italians thought we were all retreating as they were out wringing their hands. Anyway we went over to Naples again. We went into positions around Cassino and mount Kiro, and we had a couple of bumps up and down nothing serious, just to let them know we were there. Then one day forty sappers were called out and this, I shall not speak his name otherwise I will start spitting, and he said "we got a good job for you lot you are being transferred to a division that is going to do wonders" somewhere I don't know where at the particular time, he said "you are the best sappers we have got!" Bullshit, bullshit, bullshit! We knew we were going to be in for something very strong as you only get rid of the "good" sappers when you want them to get killed. We went down to just outside Naples, you could see the activity going on Naples, landing craft, and I thought where the hell were we going, are they going to open a second front. There was a lot of activity going on Cassino before we left it.

We got on to trunks and put our kits in. Everyone carried sandbags full of food, and then we were off to Naples. Another thing happened. There were nippers going round with cards Nettuno, well Nettuno was alongside Anzio. The codename for us was Shingle, I thought that was a lucky name, it means the beach. In any case it was a beach as we found out on the landing craft that we took from Naples, which wasn't very far. We went out to sea if we were going some where else and then we came back in. So we went aboard the boats.

The next thing that happened was that we went aboard a landing craft and off we went we to Nettuno which was the next town to Anzio, and apparently one of the twin towns of Anzio. Off we went to the Peter Beach and then they told us the code name shingle and you were going to land south of Rome. We got a shore and there wasn't a German in sight, apart from ones that were doing PT and guard duties. We rounded them up and they got us ready we more or less were on our own. When we landed in Anzio we were with the 1st Reconnaissance regiment, which was only lightly armoured and we stayed with them until we got as far as the road to Rome. So we came into what we thought would be a "rest camp".

Anzio (Operation Shingle)

22 January - 23 May 44

Operation Shingle was the Anglo-American amphibious assault on Anzio and Nettuno, Italy, a port located on west coast of Italy about 32 miles south of Rome. The operation was commanded by Major General John P. Lucas and was intended to outflank German forces lines of communication and by so doing to force their withdrawal from the Gustav Line.

In preparation for the assault at Anzio engineer units were put to work on the island of Corsica to create a series of deceptions (dummy dumps, landing craft etc.) to fool the Germans into thinking that the invasion target was France and not Anzio.

The deception worked, because the leading assault troops encountered few minefields, no wire, pillboxes or other obstacles, but because of the clay soil beyond the beaches the engineers were kept busy laying matting, corduroy and rock to make the area passable. 1st Division and their engineers were involved in the initial assault.

Operation Shingle - required some 374 ships of various kinds from small assault craft to Navy cruisers. Much of the Mediterranean shipping was being withdrawn to UK for the Normandy D.day landings consequently the Anzio assault was constrained by the limits of available assault and supply craft.

The landings began on January 22, 1944.

Although resistance had been expected, as seen at Salerno during 1943, the initial landings were essentially unopposed, with the exception of desultory Luftwafte strafing runs. By midnight, 36,000 soldiers and 3,200 vehicles had landed on the beaches. 13 Allied troops were killed, and 97 wounded; about 200 Germans had been taken as POWs. The 1st Division penetrated 3 km inland, the Rangers captured Anzio's port, the 509th PIB captured Nettuno, and the 3rd Division penetrated 5 km inland.

In the first days of operations the Command of the Italian resistance movement had a meeting with the Allied General Headquarters: it offered to guide the Allied

Force in the Alban Hills territory, but the Allied Command refused the proposal.

On 24 January 1944 the enemy resistance stiffened and the engineers had to take on an infantry role in the front line of the beachhead. The Guards Brigade, with 23 Field Company under command, were the floating divisional reserve and were brought ashore once the tactical picture could be seen. 23 Field Company passed us on the way to their concentration area and we exchanged cheery waves and the usual soldierly banter. They had just moved out of sight along the track when there was the frightening roar of a German fighter in low-level attack. Other soldiers heard the machine gun fire. The column was raked from end to end. It was all over in but a few seconds but 23 Field Company had a rough reception to the Beachhead. There were dead and wounded. 23rd Field Company, Royal Engineers took 80 causalities.

It is clear that Lucas's superiors expected some kind of offensive action from him. The point of the landing was to turn the German defences on the Winter Line taking advantage of their exposed rear and *hopefully panicking them into retreating northwards past Rome. However, Lucas instead poured more men and material into his tiny bridgehead, and strengthened his defences.*

Winston Churchill was clearly displeased with this action. "I had hoped we were hurling a wildcat into the shore, but all we got was a stranded whale," he said.

Three days after the landings, the beachhead was surrounded by a defence line consisting of three Divisions: The 4th Parachute Division to the west, the 3rd Panzer Grenadier Division to the centre in front of Alban Hills, the Hermann Göring Panzer Division to the east.

Further troop movements brought allied forces total on the beachhead to 69,000 men, 508 guns and 208 tanks by January 29, whilst the total defending Germans had risen to 71,500. Lucas initiated a two-pronged attack on 30 January. While one force was to cut Highway 7 at Cisterna (Battle of Cisterna) before moving east into the Alban Hills, a second was to advance northeast up the Via Anziate towards Campoleone. In heavy fighting British 1st Division made ground but failed to take Campoleone and ended battle in an exposed salient stretching up the Via Anzinate. On the right, three Ranger battalions made a daring covert advance towards Cisterna but when daylight arrived they were engaged and cut off. Of the 767 men in the 1st and 3rd Ranger Battalions, 6 returned to the Allied lines and 743 were captured.

This sergeant came up and he said, "You lot a tankie lot?" and I said, "Yeah, we are from an armoured brigade", he said, "Well you lot are going to learn how to fight now". Mmm I thought that's bloody clever, especially as the division we were joining had just come from Africa. We had been in Sicily and Italy. My mate was with us that were Jeep Middleton, and some of my other mates. We got on the boats and they told us where we were going a little place called Anzio. For 2 or 3 days we were sitting on our arses waiting to attack. The commander of the corps had merely been instructed to land, unfortunately these D-Day landings, expected to take a fortnight actually lasted three and a half months or thereabouts.

There was no action whatsoever on the beach apart from rounding up some Germans who were there. One of the officers was a fellow called Healey, Major Healey. He was Minister of Defence later on, and he was our beach master.

The officer in charge later it transpired had a black out or a stroke, which is why we didn't do anything for the first three days. Everybody was rushing around wondering what to do, and our fellow he was a cousin of the Queen, Lord LaSalle's as we were in the 24th Guards Brigade. We were more or less fitted up as a mobile striking squad and wanted to go forward. Eventually when he did go forward the Germans were waiting for us. Up in the Alban hills the Germans could see us, and there was an Armoured Division waiting for us. Our intelligence was right in the dark.

Lord LaSalle's was taken prisoner, and he was a good capture for the Germans. Anzio Rose used to broadcast and she was gloating her head off from Rome. We used to pick it up, we were not supposed to but we did. They used to give us a list of the lads that had been taken prisoner.

Suddenly we got an officer or a senior NCO who was company sergeant major from the tank corps, eventually we got a young lieutenant he didn't reign long, and none of them seemed to know what was they were up to. In charge of us was tankie office. He was a company sergeant major and I am sorry to say was as bomb happy as a newt.

This tankie officer said "We are going to go with the Grenadier guards eventually" but it wasn't today or tomorrow or the next day. So he said "what the bloody hell are we waiting here for". When we did take off of course it was too late. We got up and there was a big notice saying so many kilometres to Rome. We then met the German armour that had come across with very heavy tanks. It was cold but not raining.

This gentleman reckoned I was a "back room lawyer" he might be right but it put me in good stead for later in life when I was a shop steward at Pompey Dockyards.

After our initial landing we now found it out that this was Anzio and Nettuno. We landed at Peter Beach and the beach master was a major in the Engineers. We landed; there were only a couple of casualties of men who had stepped on shoe mines. We moved inland, first of all we had to find a billet area and we now had guides and we were guided to Padiglione Wood. This was to be our home now for the whole time we were in Anzio and Nettuno.

We had found our echelon in the woods. We took our heavy kit off and the three of us dug out a dug out. It wasn't very much of a dug out; it wasn't until later that we started digging out properly. Because first of all we went forward as were getting quite a bit of shellfire, not much, they were just letting us know they were there.

We went through the whole phase, and we only had to cough and the artillery opened fire, and we spend most of our time in the dugout, or in trenches like they did in the first war.

We were made up of Grenadiers, Grenadier Guards, because we were in the 24th Guards Brigade now, Sappers, our sapper company, and an anti-tank company. Why we didn't get the 25-pound company I don't know. Off we went on the road, the roads were very good and the Germans hadn't blown anything.

263

As soon as we went in, two of the lads shot themselves of self inflicted wounds in their feet. They didn't go out of Anzio, they went to the field officer who patched them up and they put them in a special ward that could be seen by the Germans. That was the same for the deserters. We survived this by the skin of our teeth.

I managed to get back and into our whites car which managed to turn around and head back on the road of Anzio to Rome. Actually we heard bells in Rome I don't know if it was in my bloody head or what.

To cut a long story short our company was mustered and we re-enforced the Scots guards. The other two companies they went in with their own brigades. That day every Engineer was in the firing line and there was an unpleasant bit just after this. That wasn't too bad I mean we were wet through, we were lying in mud it was pouring with rain and the Germans had got in on our right. This was up and we were facing Flyover Bridge a very infamous name. Then the battle was going forward, backwards and forwards.

I saw the first German killed by a Grenadier Guardsman by a Bren gun, and this German was going along the road from Anzio to Rome. We were all strung along and it was a job to fire as you could hit one of your own people, as there were so many milling around. Anyway he burst this Bren gun and hit him, and I was one of them who walked over to look at the body. He had 8 or 9 bullets in him. Our beach master believe it or not was the lad on the television – cheque book and busy eyebrows, he was a major in one of our divisions, and I think Field Company's, as we were field company's now not squadrons. We toddled off towards to Rome.

We were a very democratic lot, as when the Germans hit us one of our first casualties was the present Queen's cousin, they captured him. In the brigade of guards there was one of the finest jazz musicians, trumpeter, that we had going, Humphrey Lyttleton. So as I said we were very democratic, and now as I said this was my second worst one. The Germans were coming from everywhere, the blasted tanks were everywhere. In one particular instance we

265

were fighting with the Gordon's, and we were doing all right too, and what we used to do we were laying these mine fields down in front, and of course once we got to a section that had lost some men, they grabbed us for infantry. Now we were saying "I am a gentleman of the Royal Engineers" but they were going that was that.

We made a line from the sea to the factory and from the factory area to the Mussolini's canal and from the canal to pontoon marshes. We were then told to hold on. We then found out that our commander wouldn't come out and he said "his job was to get us a shore" rather than this secondary thing. We then had a terrible time just keeping our lines going.

The next thing was - here comes the Germans. Things were pretty grim and when the infantry proved insufficient, there was 5 allied division facing 12 German divisions at the beginning. The tanks never come over in front of us they came over the back of us. They had got over the main road and this wasn't covered by anti-tank guns, we thought it was. They were behind us, but fortunately the Germans when they opened up the pontoon marshes some of the tanks went in onto soft ground and they bellied.

The only ironical thing was the Germans armour had come up the side and round the back of us and there were three German tanks in the back, but thanks to the German and Italians blowing up the pontoon marshes those tanks were bellying in the marshes and they couldn't move because water had come all over the ground and there was drizzle at this particular time as well. Anyway we had to keep away from these tanks as they could still operate their arms. Now eventually by throwing grenades from the other side of the road we manage to quieten them down, and eventually by using Truman mines we managed to blow the first tank up, this tank gave us cover to have a go at the other two tanks.

When the first tank had blown up, the second tank tried to turn around but the more he tried the deeper he got. Eventually the tracks picked up the timber and stopped. They tried to get out as they tried to get out the Gordons were firing back at them and the Scots guards who had an RP were firing across the road at them. They then put their hands up and we took them prisoner. The other tank still was half buried in wadis so all we could see was the turret. Unfortunately the turret could still go round so our fellas had to wait until the turret went the other way before they could put explosives in.

These three and we blew up one as we were one side of the road and if anyone has been to Italy the roads rose, so when you got to the other side of the road you could stand up and they couldn't see you and we could hurl these grenades at them. Eventually it didn't catch fire the tank creaked and they just bailed out. Then we ran to it, and all we had to do then was put a grenade down inside the turret, then we could hide behind that one. We brought our Bren guns up – the guards did and they started firing at this tank.

I had the privilege of getting a German teller-mine, putting a charge into the detonator and lowering it into the tank and firing it. It blew the bloody turret right off! We then came back. We were now holding our own with an American cruiser, an Italian cruiser and a British cruiser. We couldn't see much as they were out at sea and we were on flat ground, and this did give us an advantage on this particular one, not later. We used them as a datum point for one of our minefields after we recovered so much ground. We used to find something substantial like a house or a tree stump or something and that would be our datum point for when we laid our mines.

After we completed the mines in a strip along a tape, we then crawled back and done the next tape. Until the complete minefield was now set. All you had to do now is wait for some poor devil to step on them.

By this time we had a pocket full of pins. So the gentleman who was now the officer was doing his bit by doing the tape and the plan. The OR's came up and gave him the pins. He could then count the pins and then know how many mines have been put in. Then we went back, now the next phrase was culvert, this was in the vicinity of fly over bridge. We had enlarged the culvert took the water from some pontoon marshes into a section of wadi's. This is where Mussolini had emptied the pontoon marshes done a good too but the Germans had done a good job too. They blew every bloody dam that was in it

The minefield, which you had put in you then took up and then put in forward. Unfortunately you recognised people who were killed. The Germans we just rolled and put to aside and then went back to the cemetery, but our men we had to identify. In some cases we left the Germans up on top, so the Germans could recover them. We fired a fairy light up in the air so they could see and if we did see any movement we didn't bother about it. In the morning they would have taken their dead away.

Anyway we then packed it with as much explosives as we could. Now one of the tasks was that two sappers stayed there on 24 hours and they had a datum to make sure the firing mechanism for that cache of explosives went up in the air, if the Germans had pushed and taken over our positions.

We were coming back from a field that we had been putting mines in, to protect the Grenadier Guards, and one Grenadier who had been at Dunkirk, told us that the commander at that time had said that he was very pleased with the efforts made, and would make sure that if there were any medals going, then the 1st infantry would be there.

That eventually packed up and the next one caught fire and that brought down all the fire from the Germans from the Alban Hills. For first few weeks we were playing cowboys and Indians, that's the only way I can describe it.

Unfortunately my company was decimated. We pulled out and went back to our rest area, and we found out that our Company Sergeant Major had got killed. We knew the junior officers were dead but we found two senior officers still alive. They had got out with 1 platoon. Our old man was dead.

The Grenadiers had to drop back, and this area was left for several weeks. We had to later recover the bodies of the men. A company sergeant major came up and gave us a nasty job to get the men out and bury them properly. We had to go and identify the men, and they had identity discs. We then had to wrap them up in gas capes. We put them on a Bren carrier. The cemetery had really grown up in Anzio. In the morning you could see all these white crosses that the grave recognition unit had put on. We got the bodies out, and there was a grave recognition unit that took them. I will say this the German respected this and you could see them quite clearly but they didn't shoot.

Things were very grim there and we were eventually sent in not for lifting mines or taken mines out but as a rifle company with the scotch guards.

The cruiser that saved us from going into the POW camp was the Penelope. I found this out later. Unfortunately either on their way back from Anzio or from Naples and she got torpedoed and sank. A lot of the lads on there we used to play football at Corpus Christi and Stamshaw School and they went down with it and drowned. I found this out after the war. As the lads that went down was the next door neighbour of my wife in Wilson Road. The two boys I went to school with were Max and Oliver

HMS Penelope was torpedoed off Anzio with the loss of 415 men on the 18th February 1944. She was nicknamed HMS Pepperpot as she had a number of holes from shrapnel when she was near Malta.

After two days we were relieved and we went back to what was termed as our rest area. This was at the end where most of our division had dug in. We had to dig in as a reserve line more or less. We kept most of our mines in case we had to put them out. Now we could see something else happening. On our extreme right on the road to Rome – the Anzio road was the British cemetery. One of our worst jobs was to go down to the beach and to collect what looked like bundles of dirty washing when the tide went out, and that was men from the boats that had sunk just off Anzio or Nettuno. We had to bring them ashore and the grave recognition unit had to take them to this cemetery. There were quite a lot of our men in there too, as we had lost about 500 men; I am talking about the Engineers.

The Germans claimed it was the biggest POW camp in their hierarchy, I think when we eventually did storm out we did prove them wrong, especially when they were trying to shove us into the sea. They also kept us well informed with what was happening to our families in Portsmouth, very graphic pamphlets they used to shoot over, "The South Coast Burns", things like that. I used to collect them and of course they were very handy for removing the brown battle stains off of our underpants.

I will say this the Germans that faced us at Anzio, contrary to what the propaganda says were the most professional soldiers had ever saw. If they were ready on the beaches on Normandy then they would have had a baptism of fire. The only thing in our favour is that we kept the division down and we got a ashore with out too much hassle. This is most of the British army Patten would have been a better general there rather than the one we had. That was that.

In fact once in Italy we were actually talking to the Italians from Nettuno on the telephone and when we took over what we call the factory area, one of the fellows rang up using the phone the German officers had left behind and he got straight into a German officers place. That was soon cut off though once they knew who they were talking to, anyway just goes to show you what you could do in the war.

The next thing we moved in to try and complete this mine fields, and we gave them numbers. Now we came into contact with the engineers we were going to be with the 23rd field company, although at this point we were working separately. We put some mines down in front of the Scots Guards. Then it was very confused for a few minutes or few hours don't know what, I was a prisoner of war.

Unfortunately one of our officers, I don't know who he was, got shot through the head. We became stretcher bearer, we put him on it and we saw this jeep with a red cross on it. We walked towards it, away from where we were and in the wadis towards Flyover Bridge. There was a doctor and he said "I am a German and what's wrong with him?" we said "this officer has been shot in the head". He looked at him and said "he is dead and you two are in the bag".

I looked at my mate which was Jeep, and there were a lot of ships firing. I think it was the Penelope, the Aurora, an American cruiser and an Italian cruiser. These were supporting the landing. A shell came up the road and it hit this tank and it just about disappeared. I had this Sten gun which I had put on the stretcher. Jeep couldn't take his rifle off but he had dropped it on the ground.

I had nothing you could see, so Jeep took the officers revolver which was on the stretcher. Another salvo came and this was the funniest thing if it wasn't so serious. About 80 men ran for the wadis. Now the wadis were occupied by the remnants of my company. So when the Germans dived in they were in the bag. So from me being in the bag they were in the bag. We had about 30 Germans and there were about 60 of us.

We were a bit shocked by this, but otherwise standing up. The Germans that ran with us, was now in our bag. We marched them to the side of the road. Told them to take their hats and helmets off and put their hands up. We walked them along the road which they could be seen, that ended that day. We then had a smokescreen come across and we couldn't tell who was who. There were whistles blowing and guns going off. Anyway they now had organised relief, we had been in three or four days. When I told my wotsname he said "so you are alright then", "yeah" I said, "More than poor old wotsname – the officer".

We were wet through, not sure if it was raining though. The Germans had blown the pontoon marshes up and these wadis's drained the water into. I think it was the Grenadiers that came into relieve us. We then formed up and marched along the road back to the Padiglione woods. Now we the re-enforcement unit we were with, they stayed behind and we checked how many we had. I think we were ten men down. Then there was signals going back and forth.

There was a sergeant in it that I sure came from Pompey. In any case when we got relived another brigade came in I think it was the Irish and of course by then the Germans had had enough and pulled back. We then managed to go forward a bit and unfortunately when you go forward the mines that we had put in we had to get out and then took forward and put down. Unfortunately one sapper blew up we don't know if it was a faulty mine or a bullet hit it. It made a nasty noise. Anyway we pulled out and we went to where our kit was which was in these woods. We got some clean clothes, and this officer came over from the 23rd field company. He said "You in re-enforcements?" and we said" Yes", "Right you are now in 23rd Field Company".

It was decided that we go and join the 23rd Field Company. Ten of us each went into each platoon and one man to HQ. We were wondering what was happened, as they given us this line of battle experienced sappers with mines. As soon as we got into these companies we were told to tell the other lads what kind of other mines to expect but we wondered where the hell we were to go. My brigade – the 24th Guards Brigade consisted of Grenadier guards, the Scots guards, the Irish guards, the 23rd Field Company, and 19th Field Regiment RA.

We now found that were in the 5th Army, American Army, not the British Army, and were to go to reinforce the 23rd Field company, putting in mines, and taking mines out, removing the dead, identifying the dead, digging tunnels under the roads, and the worst thing was that we were told to dig in.

The Badge of 23rd Field company: Black horse on a red field between horizontal blue stripes. An old Field gun in yellow on upper strip and '23 RE' in yellow on bottom strip. In 1885 earned the nickname 'The Black Horse' due to black horse teams at Aldershot. Later became known as the 'Old Battery' while in South Africa. Hence the two emblems.

The Officers in Charge were in 1942 - Major J Hornby, February 1944 - Major C Ross and August 1944 - Major E V Rambush until 1952.

Field and Field Park Squadrons

The British army had two main types of Royal Engineer units in the field and these were Field Squadrons (or Companies) and Field Park Squadrons (or Companies). The two types did perform different functions.

Field Squadron/Field Company

These were the units that went onto the battlefield and did activities (mostly under fire) like building bridges, laying or removing mines, repairing roads, demolishing roadblocks and other general tasks in combat.

Field Park Squadrons/Field Park Company

These were the units that were the supply point for all materials and engineer stores, used by the Field Squadrons/Field Companies and only occasionally did they become involved with combat.

We had to take our black berets off and put on khaki berets on, don't know why. I lost mine; I don't know where that went. I didn't get one back until I got back into the UK some time.

There was another thing that happened, our sergeant; I never talked to sergeants they only talked to you not the other way round. When we were nippers we went down the front down the beach, we used to go past a little greengrocers store down near Tipner Road. We used to go down there through the allotments and down onto the beach. I am sure that that Sergeant was of that family that ran the greengrocers shop. I never asked him because as I said I didn't talk to sergeants. He did me a favour too when I was wounded and the house fell on me, he was digging me out. He was going round shouting do this, do that and do the other one.

This sergeant was a person who liked to hear himself talk, and he said tankies – that's us as we used to wear black berets in the field squadron and this was now a field company. Nothing against them they were all pretty good lads. Geordie, one of the lads that came with us, had a luger pistol which he dropped in Sicily and the firing mechanism had fallen out – the trigger, but if he used his hands and pulled the mechanism back and let it go and would go prrr and the lot would go. Anyway this sergeant was shaving by a mirror on the lorry. I looked over and I said "you shouldn't try that Geordie you will probably blow his head off". "Will I?" he said, and the he pulled it back and the mirror disappeared. We never heard anything else about being called tankies.

We managed to get a paper on Army pension and it gave the 23rd Field Company with 79 casualties, our re-enforcement one went in with 60 men we now had 30. Our 30 was now in 23 Field Company. So they first thing they did was got our hats changed, we had armoured hats – black. We got khaki hats and we made out dugout, and got all of our kit and got into clean clothes or dry clothes.

One good thing about engineers was we already had a reasonable cook house up, and water supply, which are the most things you could want. The water was ready for showering, so all we had to do was drop all of our clothes. It was cold and we just slung this water over us and we put the dry clothes onto us. There were bags of clean clothes and socks that came up. We then got ready for our dugout. We had some grub. Now when we came ashore and ditched all our clothes we had two sandbags, one sandbag was ammunition and the other sandbag was food – tinned and biscuits. We sorted out what we wanted to keep and we piled all the rest into the cook house which they had opened up.

We managed to hold the Germans but not until they had 8 or 9 attempts. They kept coming in with a fresh division. I think we had prisoners from 8 or 9 divisions. Of course we were there on our own we didn't get relieved and then Grenadiers used to leapfrog each other the Irish Guards and the Grenadiers.

First the Grenadiers came out and they were leapfrogged us. We could then re-enforce ourselves and make sure that casualties were taken to the rear and we had a load of casualties. We lost 78 men and that's dead. I was still walking about and so was Middleton but both shell shocked. Anyway we went back to the rear.

At Pantelleria and Anzio, in Anzio there was a large boarding, and the Army had put a large figure of Janc. You might remember from the Daily Mirror and it said "have you taken your mepapa cream today?" That was the drug we would take to combat malaria.

We found a place to stow our mines and the red caps making sure you were under business. Many times I had been stopped in the truck, with mines in the back to be laid. We had to stop there whilst we were under fire. We found a wreck of this esperados, a farm but we managed to get this jeep up there with a load of mines. At the back of this farmhouse there was this jeep and there were four jerry cans which were dented and two boxes, with batteries. The jeep was no good. After we had made a covering for these mines we went back to our place. I took a door as well from the jeep. The road that we took, the Watling road I think it was called was clear of everything. There was a great big German gun, which they had to abandon – it was stuck in the ground and it had wheels. I think it was 55mm, and this marked where this base was. That was where I found the matrrene, the lights, bulbs, wire, spare toolbox, and took them back. We dug our dug out with this

Jimmy Hardman and Jeep were digging the hole but I brought back a pick from the farm and it came in handy a bit later too. When we first went there we did a recce and found a railway line and this wasn't far. So whilst they were digging a hole I went up.

We never dug in much we just made a little bivout over the top. Then on the 5th or 6th night they came over and started dropping these butterfly bombs, the next day you ought to see us digging, there was digging all over the place. That's when we found and went up and got the ties from the railway and we also bought them back for the cookhouse, but being engineers they soon fixed up a shower, which was followed around by them. The water was just rainwater, once you had, and then you had to wait for the tanks to fill up again. Drinking water was different we had to use and purify the water, that's why I got a thing about them dirty bombs when we went out into the Middle East because we did find out that radioactivity could never be taken out of the water once it was in the ground it stayed there for thousands and thousands of years to the annoyance of everybody including me.

After the was these butterfly bombs came up again, my brother John and daughter bought a house in Sussex. They were doing the garden when suddenly they unearthed one. The police asked "You sure that is a bomb?" our John said "I was a bloody engineer I am sure what they are". Bomb disposal came up "you haven't been touching that have you, its still armed". They took it away and exploded it.

We then took all this gear including the seat covers they were like a cushion with a zip on and we took them all back to our dugout in the woods. Now when the jeep was near where the mines were being put in so as soon as I went up and told them what had been salvaged and gone back from the jeep outside the farmhouse. We then marched back got some grub and we started and got our stuff out and we our pickaxe we dug, I think we dug down about 4 foot down in the ground. This was all under the air raids.

We then found water would seep in, so what we did was use the jerry cans in the bottom; they were damaged anyway and couldn't be used. We put the door on top to form a floor. If anything did get in we could just empty the jerry cans out. Now at the cook house we were living on American K rations which was came in boxes and labelled breakfast, tea, dinner whatever it was and it came in big cardboard cases. The cardboard cases we used to line the walls of the dugout. The dugout we did name and we had a naming ceremony afterwards. The three of us could get in easily but in the main there was two or maybe only one in there because you had to go out tunnelling.

Taking the pickaxe we levered off the steel rail using the handle like a fulcrum. We got four ties that were wooden (there were concrete ones as well). We took them back and we laid them across the top of the shelter, well the dugout now and we laid them at an angle. We wanted a small one, which we got, and two pieces for each end.

Now we went to the cookhouse and said to the cookhouse fella, "we got our top on we can get ten ties from the railway, can we get something for that?" He said "yeah", we got the jeep and we got a trailer and we got them in no time. By this time everyone in the woods had watched us where we were going and everyone had come back and they were all getting them up but they didn't have the sort of knowledge to get them up which we did, some of them were blowing them up.

Anyway eventually we got our top cover on our dugout and where these butterfly bombs had come down had broken the trees, we then had enough branches to cover the dugout. By the time we had finished you could hardly see the dugout all you could see was some sticks and stones on top. Once we got our blankets in there we were all right. The battery was ok and they helped generate enough to get in. Also in our k rations was books and I think I read nearly every one of that American lawyer, Perry Mason, and if never had them I used to ask the anti aircraft crew and they get them for us. Then we would give them beer as they couldn't get the beer but we could, we could get the bottles, we could get quite a bit of beer.

The cookhouse staffs were exceptional and when they snare about them about they did do or didn't do. They were bloody marvellous and don't forget shells and aircraft could find anybody in Anzio. All you had to do was pull a trigger and a shell would come over or out come the butterfly bombs on top of the lads that were down there as they couldn't go anywhere. So I don't want to hear any criticism of our cookhouse lads. They did a bloody good job.

Time the cookhouse was finished you couldn't see it. It had gone right down in the ground and it had big ramps that you could drive the trucks in and so the engine in case anything came over. Now we had these air raids almost every night or every other night. Eventually you could see the anti aircraft get the plane and you would hear this great big crash in the sky and bits and pieces would fall all over the place. Don't forget the beachhead was only a very small area for an army to be ensconced in, now in that you had the British, Americans and

Canadians. This is the only time I think that they really got on well together because we were all in the same blinking boat there was no way out unless you were wounded or deserted. We saw one plane flying in a circle over Anzio, we later learned that when the pilot bailed out the plane and made sure it crashed into the sea.

They dropped these butterfly bombs. I thought they can come over tonight and we have enough protection on top of us and it bloody well did. About four landed outside and one landed where we had the toilet, and destroyed it, some of then landed on the cook house.

The next day when we were trying to clear everything from the trees. You only had to touch those things and they were off, they were like a little grenade with a couple of rings sprouting out. When they came down you heard a swoosh, and then a bang. Again you could see a big explosion up top where anti aircraft gunners on the beach head got the planes. It was fine as long as you weren't underneath.

They reinforced us with new officers; new sappers and we more of less became a company of 220 men. Now came the worst part. When everyone had got into line, each separate company put down two minefields. Right across Anzio, the Americans did it and the Canadians – we did it right across. We more or less had a continuous line of mines. This didn't alter the fact that there mines behind it and in our area, which we had to clear. This is where is became really wotsname. As we took ground and as we re-enforced ground we went up to get the mines out –our mines, Germans mines all out to keep or own minefield in tact.

Most of the men that had been dead and had been dead for some 3, 4 or 5 weeks. In our area we had to go and try and identify our own dead. Unfortunately I think I was sick about every 10 minutes whilst I was up there, I had a scarf round my face along with a camouflage net, and I could still smell it. The poor bloody devils couldn't help that. We had to roll them into gas capes and see if there are any identity disks on them and find out who they were. The officer we had carried to the side of the road, he was still there. We took him back, the jeep comes up and it was carrying 8 or 9 at a time, and we also had two jeeps and a white's car. By the time we had recovered all of our dead including some of the Scots guards, we didn't say which is which we took them back. There was a unit called the Grave recognition unit, they were the ones that dug the graves and put the crosses up with the men's names on it. They had the job of working out which one was which, and I will never ever forget those two episodes for the rest of my life.

Then we went forward right up to flyover bridge from Nettuno, right up to Padiglione woods, camp di garne and then to the flyover. Then we waited there until they had taken some more ground. Then we branched right to the bologna and then we met up with the Americans near the railway. The factory was the next phrase and we went onto the Pria and the Factory. We got up and we could see apriato and a farm, I forget then name of that one. It certainly stunk as there were animals all over the place, anyway. The fighting around the factory and flyover bridge was rather rough. The mines we put in and if we captured the ground we had to get out as mines were pretty scarce.

There were five allied divisions, there was British, American and Canadian, against twelve very good German divisions. Now if these Germans divisions had been available for the second front, I am not saying eventually that our men from the beaches would have got on they were contained in Anzio away from. The three engineer companies of which mine was in the 24th Guard Brigade were 238 field company, (this was a Scottish raised Territorial company), 248 field company (another territorial company) and my own company was the 23rd Field Company – which was a regular company. Our casualties were 253 sappers and officers. So I think that if the soldiers that landed on D – day then that as far as they were concerned was their D Day. I got a medal from the various governments; I should think that those who landed at Anzio also deserved a medal. In Anzio that was the only place where British, American and Canadian troops fought like the First World War.

We had survived, both us, the Germans and Americans were blinking exhausted. We were going back to be re-enforced in woods.

Padiglione Woods towards the beaches of Anzio. You could actually see out onto the beaches and the sea from the woods. We were shaving, and washing, and eating all at the same time with the remnants of the Scots Guards, Irish Guards and the Grenadier Guards. Suddenly a little tornado came shouting into the area, he was a catholic priest. He was having a go at them all because most of them hadn't been to church which was quite a funny thing because we couldn't. He came straight down "you are Catholics" he said, "have you been praying?" I said "Blimey I have never prayed so much in all my life".

We could hear churches in Rome, we could hear bells in Rome but they were miles away from us. Anyway he gets us all together – all the Catholics, from the different regiments that were there. Just up the road from us, or up the trees from us, was digging in the 23rd field company. After he got us organised and we went to Mass, the first time I had been for quite some time. We went and joined up with 23rd field company. They had had a terrible bashing; they were something like 97 men down. We were very welcome, but out of our 51 re-enforcements, that went into Anzio 10 were missing and most from 626 field squadron survived.

One of the sappers from the 23rd came over and said "there is a catholic priest coming, is there any Catholics here?" So we said "yeah" and he said" we are having a mass". I don't know what day it was or how long we had been in Anzio at this point.

There was quite a few from the Irish Guards, the 23rd Field Company and the other two field company's that were there. The priest who later we saw quite a lot of said mass and he said "Thank God you are all alive" and we thought it was a bit funny about God. I always thought my grandmother helped me as she was dead. If I was in a bit of untoward I would always think of her, she was the main spring of the family before she died. The other things were I said my times afterwards, and he came from Lancashire, and he was coming backwards and forwards along the line. Once of the guards putting in mines one day said "When we get to Rome father we will make you adjutant to the Pope". Actually whilst I said that, the chap who said it was in the Irish Guards but he came from London. There was also a chap there who got a VC in Africa; he was from Northern Ireland I think.

While we were having this mass with this Father, there was an air raid going on, and there was things cutting across, and the ack acks was going on. Planes were being blown up. They were trying to get our ships and cutting across the beach head to let us know they were there.

We heard the ships opening up and all the time this was going on a big gun called Anzio Annie was firing out from a tunnel, which we found out afterwards. It made a funny noise, it made two bangs and then whoosh and bang. Most of them were aimed at the docks were they were unloaded. There were these docks coming from the big landing craft, there were liberty ships, and warships. There was quite a collection of ships out there. You could see the shell banging down. It didn't seem to be shelling where the troops were they used to leave that to the Germans up in the Alban Hills. That was pretty hairy that was.

I used to collect was propaganda leaflets I had a good outlet for them in our cookhouse. All down the Albany Road and up to the Flyover they used to fire these shells full of these pamphlets over. When they exploded they all used to come down. We used to give it a rest before we went and picked them up. As sometimes they would start a mortar just after they came down. Then I used to go out and collect them, and sometimes the shells that had exploded. They used to come down with a funny noise and a big thump. You would go and unscrew them and take out the roll of pamphlets. These I would take back and give to our cooks and they used to give us extra food such as corned beef and stuff.

The propaganda leaflets would say things like the following:-

How you will be treated as a POW by the Germans

- *food, toilets, learn a trade, athletics, entertainment*
- *mail*
- *return home safe and sound after the war*
- *Don't get the dirty end of the stick – don't get killed.*

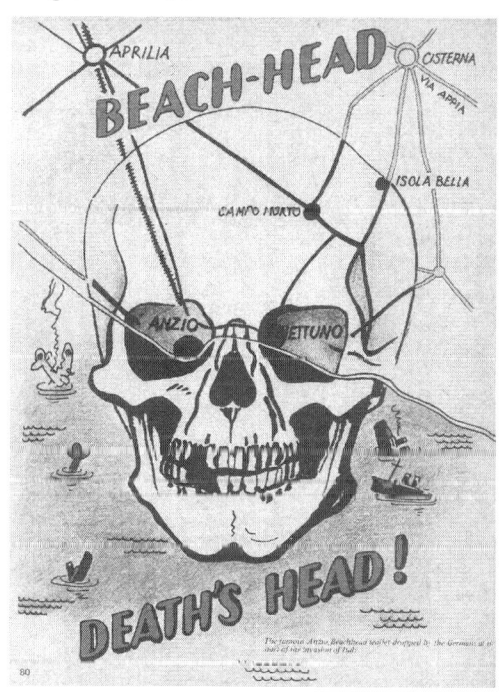

Propaganda leaflet

The officers all had maps on where the units should be and what we should be doing but actually where we supposed to be we weren't and where we weren't supposed to be we were. It was a matter of doing right wherever you were. Most of our time was spent bailey bridging, mine lifting, it wasn't until we got to Anzio that we started putting stuff in. We had the occasional Messerschmitt go over as we got up to the Sangro we got a bit more. As we now nearing bases as we were in Northern Italy, and we expected more from air craft.

The three officers that we had – the two genuine ones were really first rate people and I did say that one of them was the son of one of my employers in Pompey dockyard. He was an electrical officer in the Royal Navy and I used to take messages up to him when I was a yard boy. It was in my pay book that stated that I shouldn't receive any money from pay master until the pay master had been informed that I was receiving my money made up from being a civil servant. It didn't make much but it gave me a bit more than most of the lads.

We went in to re-enforce the Scots Guards, we went in as a rifle company. Unfortunately we got surrounded and we had the heaviest casualties and we lost two thirds of our men. When we got back we soon got up to strength with re-enforcements from other units and us then started to our great tunnelling experience. A task I didn't mind was tunnelling under the road.

There were some sappers that were Welsh miners and they showed us how to do these tunnelling. The timber came in and we had to cut this timber into four and made them into a box with no bottoms. We did four a night or four a shift day and night. That was our mine thing until we got to a concrete sort of culvert and we had to bash our way through that. In the end we used to store our explosives and ammunition so if the Germans did come through we could blow it. I think we did four of them before we got the flyover. In front of the flyover was the factory, and our job was to get to the factory. You could get to the factory if there was no water in it easily but it appeared it was drains that went into this factory. I am not sure if it was tomatoes but it was a big factory. In fact a couple of times we were underneath and the Germans were up top. A lot of our lines went under ground and out, you could get out up top. Of course I was a lot slimmer then.

After that we were then digging tunnels, digging trenches, blowing holes in the ground so guns could go in, and of course blowing down houses in Anzio, and most them were down by the time we broke out and made into roads. These roads we built in the woods under cover and the tunnels allowed the men to move about without being spotted or have a rest or dry clothes, as all the time this was happening it was raining, and snowing. Smoke was coming over from Vesuvius one time.

Otherwise everything was all right. I stayed alive, I told you about the kit inspection, there was bother, they talk about the mutiny at Salerno, and all the lads were talking about mutiny. But I said, "Look here, if this Salerno business was true, then it would be best to carry on and argue afterwards". So I said "right" I was senior sapper so I said this" when I was in the 8th army we all heard something nasty – the mutiny at Salerno. So I said to them all "call them all the names you want to but do it" and we did it. The junior officers didn't think much of it but somebody said that and I don't know but all the engineers done it.

That's what they did, and the final part of my bit, we heard through the lavatories was about the mutiny at Salerno. Troops come over from North Africa, ex-wounded from hospital being sent to units that had just come out and their own units were going home. If it carried on from there we had no relief, we got put on a boat at Taranto and we didn't know if we were going home or somewhere else. We found out afterwards we going to the Middle East, anyway that were another story.

The only highlights as far as I was concerned were the tunnelling through the roads, which gave us quite a lot of rest, and the nightly talk of the Germans from Rome of the woman giving the prisoners, our boys, numbers. So we then found out if our mates were alive.

Between us, the Americans and the Canadians and the Germans - a flock of sheep in no mans land all the time I was there, and when I went back to fetch something with one of our officers in a jeep. They were then carolled by one of the farms which were there, it was in ruins. The farmer said that they had born the sheep, the flock or whatever it was, and it exactly the same as when he left it. I don't think any of the troops would have shot them, they would do chickens – we found a lot of them but not the sheep.

On the beach head was an American bomber had come from North and had been damaged. It used to circle the beach head and every so often out came a man with a parachute of course. Everybody would wait anxiously to see if he fell into Allied hands or German hands. I think most of them did, two of them landed up near us. Of course that was something that happened.

We then went to a cinema; yeah, we had a cinema there. The Americans helped us, they brought up all their equipment and we dug this blasted big hole in the ground, we sandbagged the top part of it and then two companies at a time could go and see a film at a time. Yeah this was in Anzio. Anyway we were complimented on that and the other one was to build a secret road through the woods.

This was where most of the troops were billeted and so we used to knock the big villas down at Anzio, American trucks again used to come up and we used to do a section of road right to where we used to call the factory area. We didn't go as far as the factory area was but by a series of trenches – zig zag trenches you could get to the side of the road. One day we used the rubble from one villa and amongst the rubble we found the body of a baby. That shook everyone up.

What we had to take our mepropane, there was talk of mutiny although we felt like it. The army is very uncaring, I will put it gently. They even took away the medals and decorations of the men who were involved in the mutiny. Don't know If they gave them back or pardoned, I am blowed if I could find anything out. We had an O group once in Madeira, we used to have these O groups, we were told ask anything, I asked them "Is there any truth in this business of the mutiny at Salerno?" This intelligence officer "No I haven't heard of that I will try and find out".

I never found out though, I don't know if it is true now.

We now heard a bit more about the mutiny at Salerno. I think they went back to North Africa to where we had our court martial. After they shot the sergeant, I got exonerated quickly. We heard that there were about 200 people involved including three senior NCO's. They were all sentenced and the three sergeants to death, but eventually it were passed that they just had to go in prison. I thought it was one of the stupidest things that the army had ever done, but it had repercussions in Anzio. Just to think what the Army could to do. One day we were told to have a kit inspection of course a lot of the lads were going to say go and jump. I said "Look we heard about this mutiny business at Salerno, do as your told and complain afterwards", and that is what we did.

We had to get REME tank recovery truck to drag this tank – small tank and we removed the explosives as it was full of made up charges with like slabs of metal which looked like chocolate so when it did go off, I think some of these things the IRA have used in Northern Ireland. In any case our officer got a medal for it or something.

At no time during the whole of the 4 month-period of the Battle of Anzio was any place out of range of enemy artillery and, no matter where, one was liable to be shelled whether in Anzio town, on the beaches, in the woods or at the front; everyone was in a forward area; there was no rear area. Ammunition and petrol dumps were prime targets and to see one of these go up was quite something - pyrotechnics galore! Anzio town was specially selected to receive the attentions of "Anzio Annie". The Germans are good at very big guns!

There was a big gun called "Anzio Annie", it was a big siege gun. Periodically it would trundle out to perform its party-piece, which was to hurl a shell weighing a quarter of a ton at the beachhead distant a mere 20 miles. It could deliver its lethal missile, if persuaded by a team of 10 men, over distances up to 38 miles! Its target was mainly Anzio town, which it steadily reduced to piles of rubble. It used to fire in the hope of hitting, it hit quite a few too, our destroyers or liberty ships or these duck taps, and of course we would have to run under shellfire but you could hear this one coming. It sounded like it was a double barrel thing; you would hear weee bang weee BANG. The second bang was a nasty one because that went up in the air.

Most of the shellfire from Anzio Annie you used to hit the, along the beach there were marvellous houses. We used to shelter in them sometimes and of course there were all these shops and all the stuff they would use for holidays. Spread all over the place.

I picked up two small vases Nettuno and Anzio. I carried them around in my ammunition pouches right until the end of the war. Unfortunately the Nettuno one smashed. I got the Anzio one here and its in the cabinet here. Then I was talking about these lads who were unfortunately killed. We used to take them back; there was an officer in charge. And I found out that he was from Portsmouth and he was from one of the funeral directors. When he came out of university and of course he was hooked up with the Grave Recognition Unit. That was that.

German K-5 Railway gun "Leopold" (aka "Anzio Annie")"Anzio Annie" was the name used by the Allies for a pair of German K5(E) railroad guns that shelled the Anzio beachhead during World War II. The Germans named them "Robert" and "Leopold".

The guns were captured on 7 June 1944. Robert was partially destroyed by the gun crew before they surrendered and Leopold was also damaged but not as badly. Both guns were shipped to the U.S. Aberdeen Proving Ground, (Aberdeen, Maryland) where they underwent tests. One complete K5 was made from the two damaged ones, and "Leopold" remains on display to this day at the United States Army Ordnance Museum located on the Aberdeen grounds.

By now both sides had realised that no decisive result could be achieved until the spring and reverted to a defensive posture involving aggressive patrolling and artillery duels whilst they worked to rebuild there fighting capabilities. In anticipation of events in the following spring, Kesselring ordered the preparation of a new defence line, the Caesar C line, behind the line of beachhead running from the mouth of the river Tiber just south of Rome through Albano, skirting south of the Alban Hills to Valmontone and across Italy to the Adriatic coast at Pescara, behind which 14th Army and, to their left, 10th Army might withdraw when the need arose.

March and April 1944

With both Allied and German forward positions static, conditions at Anzio resembled the trench warfare on the Western Front of the First World War. Except when some movement on either side provoked a sniper's bullet, or a burst of machine gun fire, or brought down either mortar or artillery fire, the front lines in daylight were still and quiet. With darkness, the beachhead came to life. Patrols went out or were beaten off; trenches and fox-holes repaired; food, ammunition and supplies brought forward; the wounded were evacuated; the dead buried and relief's carried out. Bursts of harassing fire from time to time, and even flares, would suddenly put a stop to all movement and activity.

Unlike the Western Front of the First World War, there were no rear areas as such, and at Anzio, no one was safe. The whole beachhead area was within range of artillery fire and the bulk of VI Corps' casualties during the period were caused by artillery fire and air raids. Gerry used a wide range of guns from the deadly 88mm to a giant 280mm railway gun, which the troops nicknamed 'Anzio Annie' or the 'Anzio Express'. The Luftwafte even used rocket powered, remote controlled 'Glider Bombs' that were dropped by attacking aircraft and guided on to the shipping, anchored off shore.

A new Nazi weapon showered them from the skies - a nasty device called a Butterfly Bomb. This was a small canister of explosives from which sprouted vanes causing it to rotate and fall slowly, rather after the style of sycamore seeds one sees twisting down from the tree in the Autumn. These nasty bombs lay silent and inert on the ground or perhaps in long grass or undergrowth but the tiniest movement would detonate the device causing the loss of a foot, blindness or other injury. From the German point of view these were an efficient *weapon as a wounded man is more of a liability than a dead one.*

Quite a bit of the surrounding area was low lying and swampy. The Italians before the war had heavily drained the land, in an attempt to improve the farming. There were virtually no 'cross country' routes and most of the traffic was restricted to the highways. This was also true for the tanks. There were no pitched tank battles because the tank formations were restricted to half a dozen or so and had to operate using the roads. So it was that the Royal Engineers were called upon to provide 'hard core' for repairing damaged roads and for making new ones.

The British 1st and 5th Divisions were about 3,600 men below establishment, owing to a shortage of infantry reinforcements. For this reason, they were to be used only in a holding role, and were not to be used north of the Tiber, until reinforced. On 22nd May, these two divisions were placed directly under the command of the American Fifth Army.

Despite Alexander's overall plan for Diadem requiring VI Corps to strike inland and cut Route 6, Clark asked Truscott to prepare a number of alternatives and be ready to switch from one to another at 48 hours notice. Of the four scenarios prepared by Truscott Operation Buffalo called for an attack through Cisterna, into the gap in the hills and to cut Route 6 at Valmontone. Operation Turtle on the other hand foresaw a main thrust to the left of the Alban Hills taking Campoleone, Albano and on to Rome. On May 5 Alexander selected Buffalo and issued Clark with orders to this effect.

Anzio Poem

Another one that is in my mind is a poem that came over the air; I don't know who the author was. We had plenty of walkie talkies – the Americans saw to that, and I will just read it. I still got it on the signal paper my mate said to go slowly which he did and I wrote it down, and here it is.

Anzio Beachhead

When Machine guns stop their chatter

And cannons stop their roar

And you are back in dear old Blighty

In your favourite pub once more

And the small talk is all over

And the war tales start to flow

You can stop them all by saying

Of the fight at Anzio

Let them Brag about the desert (actually we were there as well!)

Let them brag about Dunkirk

Let them Brag about the jungle

Where the Japanese did lurk

Let them talk about their campaigns

And their medals until they are red

You can put the lot in silence

When you mention the beachhead

You can tell all your setbacks

And our own fortress with the Huns

They used to ask us out to breakfast

As they rubbed against their guns

You can tell of night patrolling

They know nothing of that at home

You can tell them that you learned it

At the beach head south of Rome

Now as we go down to the breakout, as I already told you on this tape. We lined up, we were told the Tiber was our first and Civitavecchia, a little port near Rome. Then we were to swing back round to Rome itself. Now there is a little bit of an argument going on about the war near Rome. It wasn't, as far as we were concerned Rome was an open city. The Italian partisans saw to that. But Mark Clark was keen to get there. He swung his army back into Rome and cut off the Germans. Our people came up highway 6 before we pushed out and we had to achieve in case something else didn't materialise. Now everyone would have thought that would have been the second front, but there were other things to consider as well. All the landing craft had to be back in the UK by a certain time. These were the landing craft we used - di vittles and Landis, and I think that Mark Clark is on the record for saying the same thing, and that he was frightened of the casualties on the second front if we never took Rome. Anyway we took Rome the day before the landing. Also the casualties of the Germans. If we hadn't landed at Anzio, those troops would have been ready to face our troops instead of engaging us. Their casualties of the Germans were really high and so were ours. When it was all put down on paper.

A quote updated from Shakespeare's Henry V that was said about Anzio: -"Then will he strip his sleeve and show his scars. And say 'These wounds I had on at Anzio.'"

Anzio Breakout

We made our fire out of ammunition boxes and shell cases. Some of them had made cigarette cases out of the bottom of the shells and put a small aircraft on which I have still got. It's somewhere in the house and the next thing was, before we went up the road. The King of England – King George was going to come and our company was told to get back there to Anzio. We didn't go right back there but up to the Alban Hills there was a place there to the side. There was a place called a parrioo???? that had taken hundreds of lives trying to take. The king of England was given a pair of binoculars that we had thought had come Pantallerio, and I thought at the time my pair of binoculars that I got from Pantallerio were at the bottom of the Mediterranean, including a lot of notes of lira. I did have a lot of notes of lira as we used to carry them around – I was a millionaire lira, until that fateful accident when our landing craft.

I don't know if this is true but there was an explosion when the king was looking at the positions where we were on Anzio. We heard a cry "sapper, sapper". As Sappers up we went they had surrounded the party and we swept into the road to make sure there was nothing underhand. It may have been to let us know that patrols were about. Anyway there was a bang. I heard the bang and I said what's that then.

This was on the Albania Road but we also dug zigzag trenches like they did in the First World War from just behind the gun to the front, which was where you could see the factory area, hope you can make some sense out of this Al, and that is all now.

The next phrase I was talking about this road, now this road had to stop when we were more or less in view of the Germans. When the big push came to go we kept a lot of the trucks loaded up with scrap from the big villas I was talking about down in Anzio and Nettuno and they stayed in reserve ready to go forward and to complete the road into Carrigeta. It was all across the countryside and then when the final push come of course you had something hard to keep your tracks on especially Bren carriers, which we used right up to the break out and up to the Tigre.

We could see the work we had done proven to be very beneficial to us the tunnels in the road you could see troops coming out of them in long lines ready for the assault on the Tigre. They come out like ants in ant hill and also the road we built through the woods was chock a block now with Bren carriers and armoured cars on their way to the port of Rome, Civitavecchia.

Now at the side of the road was a great big steel manhole cover, which you could pick up and go down and you were then amongst telephone wires that went into the factory. This was either a spaghetti or tomato tin factory. One time when our infantry was taking it we were there as well you could hear the Germans upstairs and us downstairs or vicky versa we were upstairs and they were downstairs. All according to how fast you could move. When I am talking now it was in our hands (the factory) and I think it was the grenadier guards, anyway, we then established a minefield out front. Everything now was who goes first, do we have a go or the Germans have a go.

I can now talk about the break out, now it was obviously that the Americans didn't let the British go into Rome, although most of our fellas was in there and they did negotiate with the Italian partisans that Rome would be an open city. Our orders on the breakout was to go straight down to the Tibre.

Truscott's planning for Buffalo was meticulous: British 5th Division and 1st Division on the left were to attack along the coast and up the Via Anziate to pin the German's 4th Parachute, 65th Infantry and 3rd Panzergrenadier in place whilst the U.S. 45th Infantry, 1st Armoured and 3rd Infantry Divisions would launch the main assault, engaging the German 362nd and 715th Infantry Divisions and striking towards Campoleone, Velletri and Cisterna respectively. On the Allies' far right the 1st Special Service Force would protect the U.S. assault's flank.

In the afternoon of May 25 Cisterna finally fell to 3rd Division who had had to go house-to-house winkling out the German 362nd Infantry, which had refused to withdraw and, as a consequence, had virtually ceased to exist by the end of the day. By the end of the 25th, 3rd Infantry were heading into the Velletri gap near Cori and elements of 1st Armoured had reached within 3 miles of Valmontone and were in contact with units of the Herman Göring Division, which were just starting to arrive from Leghorn. Although VI Corps had suffered over 3,300 casualties in the three days fighting, Operation Buffalo was going to plan and Truscott was confident that a concerted attack by 1st Armoured and 3rd Infantry Divisions the next day would see his troops astride Route 6.

The final move on Rome On the evening of May 25 Truscott received new orders from Clark via his Operations Officer, Brigadier Don Brand. These were, in effect, to implement Operation Turtle and turn the main line of attack ninety degrees to the left. Most importantly, although the attack towards Valmontone and Route 6 would continue, 1st Armoured were to withdraw to prepare to exploit the planned breakthrough along the new line of attack leaving 3rd Division to continue towards Valmontone with 1st Special Service Force in support. Clark informed Alexander of these developments late in the morning of May 26 by which time the change of orders was a fait accompli.

Rome finally fell on 4th/5th June 1944. The four months that had elapsed since the Anzio landings had seen some bitter fighting. But Operation Overlord overshadowed the capture of Rome, the D-Day landings in Normandy on June 6th. The main importance of the Italian campaign lay in the support that was given to the Normandy landings by the effective holding down of 25 German divisions in Italy, that could have been employed in France. "To force the enemy to commit the maximum number of divisions in Italy at the time Overlord is launched."

On the way down to the Tibre we went past a farmhouse and the Americans were in there as we were on the edge of our division and an American division. They were examining one of these in the farmhouse we had a look at and one of them come up against us and it flies off a bridge and its now on its way back to the Uk. They were getting ready go back to America. There were two tanks in this courtyard. Then we got past and we got down to the river. We were held up first of all; by a German SP gun but we had mortars. I did tell you a little bit about this when we were going across the Sangro.

This time we knew how to fire it, we had one, if you fire it level the bloody fins come back at you. This one we lobbed as eventually the Germans ran away, as they saw a load of troops coming.

The road we were coming on was absolutely packed with Americans that had come over with this division. We then went right down to the Tiger and we come to a bridge now. This bridge we should have not touched we should have been further down the river towards the coast, as our divisions were going across that. We knew this but we went across it. As we were sappers we ran across the bridge. Every so often they had a bomb on the bridge but our lorry just went around until we got to the other side and there on the other side was the biggest bomb I have ever seen. It was as big as a boiler but the wires that were coming out of it we cut and then we got to the beach. We signalled everyone across the river and then we stopped.

First of all the Italian partisans come up and there was a sign saying Roma so many kilometres away. It was too big for me to collect, but these partisans wanted us to go into Rome. Of course we had this order that no British were allowed into Rome and in case our company commander was on the blower and he was trying to bring all the sappers down there as they were now facing an attack by armour. They wanted everyone down there and that was at port of Rome.

In the port of Rome eventually when we did capture it as went back along the river was the zoo. You could hear these animals growling, screaming and yelling but fortunately there was lot of horses that had been killed and the Army and the staff at the zoo dragged the dead animals into the zoo for the animals to eat, which they did. Then we got an order that Mark Clark had entered Rome well there was nothing really.

The American 5th Army instead of going and cutting Highway 6, went straight into Rome, which they had no need to do, as the partisans were already holding it. We went across the Tiber, and stuck close to a German division, and pushed through to what was called the port of Rome, we then pushed on for a further 20 miles and then stopped. We were then ordered back and entered Rome itself and we got re-equipped.

Rome was an open city that partisans were in control and I think this son of the New Zealand commander Craybourne was there as well so Britain was well represented. Another division came through us, I think it was the 5th division not quite sure now. We received the glad tidings that because of our fighting in Anzio, our commander, an American commander, we had a new one as they found the old one in the catacombs – he had a nervous breakdown, had given us the privilege of being garrisoned in Rome for 3 to 4 weeks. We packed everything up and we went in there. We went into what was the Olympic stadium and that became the divisional command of the 1st British Infantry.

After two or three days of scrubbing, cleaning all of clothes and changing all of our clothes, we got new boots and getting new transport. So we moved out of the stadium and moved into a housing estate, which they moved all the tenants out and we took straight over.

All for this lot I have not said anything apart from that nasty episode when we did lose a lot of men at Anzio and we did lose a lot of men going across the Sangro River. I have not said much about it except them two points. Both of them it was bloody inefficiency that got them killed. We couldn't do anything about because we were bloody privates. To go back on my father when they made rather stupid attack, because he was with the Australians and New Zealanders so I don't know if that is me as a survivor of the 2nd world war in their parade in ANZAC day, bearing in mind how close my father, and the Australians and the New Zealanders and there were Indians on that last day before that evacuation and it was Ringwood where they were re-cuperated and he used to tell my mother and his sister about how terrible it was on that little place.

Unfortunately I was the same as him, I was an unpaid corporal and he was an unpaid corporal, he left Egypt to go to the Dardanelles and I left Egypt for all points west and east - Sicily and Italy and then I went back there, knocking about there with terrorism.

Rome

I think we got to the back of Rome on the 4th June and it wasn't until the 6th June. I think we beat them but our effort went unrecognised. Our few months on the beaches of Anzio were greater than their few days and weeks on the beaches of Normandy. As the Lily Marlene song was heard, I heard the last one from Rome, which gave so many prisoners names and that always finished with Lily Marlene. As I said before the 1st infantry division were given Rome to be patrolled by the British 1st Infantry Division, they way we fought at Anzio. It wasn't very easy for the engineers in the 1st Infantry Divisions the casualties were very high.

All this went on until we were ready to go out and have a real dabble for Rome. We also knew that something else was going to happen but not a lot of people have said anything about this. They have gone on about the d day this and the D-day that there is only one D-Day as far as everyone is concerned over here, and there was more than that over there. Now we were ready, we were told we had to do this – take Rome, because if the other one failed they would have something to tell people that we had done, but this was never put over. Normandy took pride of place on every other occasion.

All the divisions were lined up with the Americans to the left and the Canadians Special Brigade to the extreme right. When we got ready our job – the British job was to straight up to the Tiber, across the Tiber and straight round to the back of Rome. There were a lot of Germans trapped there including in the Rome Zoo. Some of the animals had been eaten, but there was some there. German tanks were in sight of there. In fact we had a big tank battle before we managed to get behind Rome.

The Americans had to go straight up onto, I think Highway 6. Then straight into Rome, it was a question on where you were in Anzio. It was just fortunate for them that they were there. The Canadians went straight out and then cut across to Highway 6. The American General was so pleased on how the British handled themselves that he gave us the first allied division to garrison Rome.

On this side of the Mediterranean in Anzio, we were in the American 5th Army, the Americans treated us really good and as I said they gave us the garrison of Rome. Several things stick in my mind, when we kicked off from our start point the cemetery which was on our right, this was in our rest area, we could just see, it was just getting light and we could see the white crosses and I noticed how big it was now compared to when we first dug in. I don't know how many men were in that cemetery I had another look at it from the Alban hills and blimey what the Germans couldn't see was wasn't worth knowing. It was a bloody miracle that we survived and if it wasn't for our Navy ships I don't think we would of.

Audience with the Pope

8th June 1944

The Garrison of Rome was one of my highlights and one thing we did there was all Catholic troops in the 8th and 5th Army was going to the Vatican to see the Pope. There was an order from company sergeant, he was the gaffer and all Catholics in 8th Army, 5th Army, colonial forces, were to go to parade in Rome, in the Vatican City, well in Rome, we were going to march along. Alexander himself a catholic, had organised or had said that all British troops in Italy should go for an interview or a blessing with the Pope. We had privilege position and marched behind the Argyll's with a piped band. They had their full pipe band they had flown out from the UK, I think Aldershot. The RAF flew a Dakota and brought it all out and they looked a picture. The only thing is the troops didn't have any kilts but the band did and they looked bloody smart. I was surprised about how many Catholics were in the 23rd Field company. The Italians were wondering about all us atheists.

Now we got to the station in Rome, the lads formed up, of course we were now in the 23rd Field Company. A young voice that I hadn't heard for a long time, a Welshman said, "Freddie Britt, Jimmy Middleton I thought you buggers was dead". He was the youngest recruit for to the 626 field squadron when we across to Cassino before I went to Anzio. So I said "Taff, what's up?" I forget his second name. When he first came to the squadron he could hardly speak English all he knew were the commands and he learnt English the proper way from the troops from us.

This is what he told us he was reinforcement to the 626-field squadron somewhere in Italy when we first landed. About 30 of them came. He said we didn't know you people had left the squadron until our turn came up now the reinforcements didn't go to Anzio but they did go to another unit and he said on such and such a date 626 went home with the 4th armoured brigade which was the 7th armoured division.

This is where I learnt that the 51 sappers that left 7th Armoured Division at Cassino went to Naples and went straight

329

into Anzio as re-enforcements, as battle experienced Sappers, if there was ever was a word like that. I don't think you could ever get battle experienced just fright.

Well Taff said "when you lot gone all the men that had joined 4th Armoured Brigade, 7th Armoured Division, was the next lot and what they did for us they sent us 22nd Armoured corps", so that meant that all the lads that didn't confirm and all the lads that had just joined had now left, and now they left for the UK and went for D-Day. Now he tied up everything he was not the only one there, there were two others as well. They couldn't have got any satisfaction. Their D-day lasted a fortnight. Ours lasted three bloody months. So we were punished not once but three times, and then we formed up.

We had a whip round afterwards and we gave Taff and some of the other lads some souvenirs from that farmer and from the Americans. We said have a nice long drink on us in fact we had some very good drink but it wasn't with us it was back at our billet.

We formed up and I never knew that there were so many Catholics in the British

Army. One of our best bands the Argyll's, the people in Rome turned out in their thousands. The Ghurkhas were policing it and us as well, and they were really smart; and so were we, we had our best shorts on, our best shirts, red belts, no weapons. We marched behind the Argyll's. It took about a couple of hours to get into the Vatican City, up the steps and into St Paul's and we saw the big pictures on the wall.

One of scotch regiments even sent home and had their pipe band flown out for this big do, and I tell you what I have never seen so many Italians, if the Germans had come over they would have had a field day, but as I say Rome at this point was getting like an open city. We marched down, to the railway station and there was a great big square in front of us and this was filling up with the troops. Our pipers of the Argyll's led us, the 1st infantry division into the Vatican. One of the most stirring songs I have ever song and I have song it too, "the land of my fathers". I think it shook everybody including the Italians who thought we were a bunch of atheists.

Anyway everything now went according to plan, we formed up, marched through the city, went to see the Pope – Pope Pius. We had to march to the basilica just outside Vatican for mass, and then we marched inside the Vatican and in the main hall where Pope Pius came through. I held up all my photographs of my wife, Alan, my uncle's children, my mother (of course) for his blessing, out we came. I held them up and pope blessed them all as he went past. I have got a small little medal they gave us when we left. That was one of our highlights. The other highlight was when we went into Rome we were given these leaflets on how to behave. This was in the Rome Allied soldiers souvenir guide. We were British soldiers we knew how to behave. We were gentlemen. Then we got a photograph on the steps, went back to the Olympic Stadium in Rome.

The Pope received General Mark Clark for a private audience and spoke to him for 10 minutes. Later that day Pope Pius X11 received 700 American and British soldiers in the Hala Clementina. Soldiers in dusty khaki and hob nailed boots made a strange sight after intense fighting in Rome from the allies. The pope blessed them in English " We bless all you here in person, and we send our blessing to your loved ones at home. We pray that God in his love and mercy will be with you always. Goodbye; bless you all". Then there was clapping and cheering and some soldiers went forward to kiss the Pope's hand. Each soldier was given a small rosary as a keepsake.

Water point and Rome

There was another little mine episode, which happened, after we got pulled out of the line, still in the 5th American Army and we went back to Rome. There we were put into the Olympic stadium of the Italians and the thing that struck me, all in the lobby of this place was great big panels in marble denoting the prowess of the Roman legions and of course Britain was there as well. Just after that the company went out, to a corporation estate, so our transport went out onto the grass and got all our equipment out. Suddenly our section officer came up, marvellous fellow, and said "lads you got a job on". This lance corporal just came out of the Uk, we are forming a water point and its about 8 miles from here.

We had to make sure that the water was safe that meant that some of the chemicals were still working and the end ones but you could top up and so we were open for business but there was one problem on the far side was a farm, quite a large road, there were lovely roads in Italy, and this was quite clear but there was mines up either side, although we didn't check then but we knew these were German mines.

We later found out there were a few and unfortunately they were on the opposite side and there was a double main road past us where we got the water point and we made a road that was running past us towards the road that was past the farm so the transport that was coming from Rome could turn round go along and go back. Well we checked it and we were open for business and in no time the word went round that there was a water point there and up come all the odds and ends from the 5th Army, from the American 5th Army, mostly American and two British divisions. We then filled all their jerry cans as we emptied one tank so we topped it up with another one and then pumped water in to the end one so there was a continuous stream of water fit for drinking. Of course you still had to boil it.

Now we said we have a look at these mines now if with the concentration of these trucks Jerry – the luftwafte – they were still active found us they would scatter and we were frightened that some of them might hit the minefield anyway we found about 7 on these verge, the opposite verge, we lifted these, they were just teller mines. We removed the detonators, now these were a problem as we had no means of either detonating away from the mines or making them safe we put them aside but then one of the water people came up – American – we could tell by his badges that he was a combat engineer and we explained as he had been in Anzio with us "that's alright buffle them up and we can explode them back there, where our camp is" So that is what we did, we kept the mines because you can use the explosive to brew up your own fire and so we emptied them, and we told our officer who used to come up with our grub and he took those back for training "you get anymore" he says "lets have them especially different type".

So this is what we did but then the farmer came up who owned the land he couldn't use the land where the mines were and according to the signs quite a long range of them and ended with a sort of building which animals used to be kept in and in the case which the Germans had, we didn't need it. "So" he says "you are engineers if you clear those mines for me so I can get my cattle from this field to the next one I would be very appreciative" I said before when I got weighed off for a warrant, well this is where it was going to pay me back so I wouldn't lose any money, well I already lost the money but this is what we did. In-between filling up these tanks we cleared the mines we used bayonets there was, you could almost, see them so there was no danger. All you had to worry about that there was nothing underneath them, which we did. We then removed the mines.

Eventually we had about 30 teller mines, well bayonets are good at going forward but there were the odd bits and pieces you could have missed so when our officer next came up. We told him, there is quite a few here, we got all the detonators out but as we said we cant fire them, we have nothing to fire them. We had been keeping the explosive for brewing up which you knew about.

Incidentally this officer was a member of one of the big dance bands, lived in London and another unfortunate thing happened to him, anyway I will tell you later, as it concerns this. We knew that this officer had a German sub machine gun, when we cleared the mines the Italian said there was quite a lot of gear left behind in the house, they were frightened to go in there, anyway we checked but there was nothing in there. No booby traps but there were boxes full of red devils.

I used to doctor red devils which were small hand grenades which the Germans and Italians used to use. In any case none of them were armed, and I used to sell them to the Americans, not so much for money, as money was not much use, but they were allowed to buy stuff from their NAAFI, and I used to exchange badges from Germans and these red devils. They used to turn these red devils into table lighters for cigarettes.

Now red devils were more in less cash in hand, all we had to do, there two parts that used screwed together – the explosive part and the firing point. Now there was a small pin you had to push down, and you twisted so that the pin went into the grooves of the screw part to lock the two parts together. You could then remove the bottom part from the top part and in there was a charge and a detonator, it was fired from a flap made of leather. You pulled that something went down, struck the explosive the detonator and off went the charge. It was only a small flash; I don't think it would have done much damage. By the time we had finished we had a huge heap of these things we had disarmed and of course we had a ready market.

As the Americans came up they would buy them. The American currency in Italy was better than military currency. The British had military currency. When we were in the American army we had American currency and we used to call gold dollars, they had a silver seal on them, which meant you could not get rid of them in the states. We could only get rid of them in PX's, the American equivalent to NAAFI.

Well as soon as they come up the first ones I got were the lads that were in the engineers. Of course so it was no use selling them so what we did was we exchanged gifts and they were quite satisfied but we also were told of all the other Americans the anti aircraft lads and the infantry and they exchanged their gold dollars for these, mind you they were disarmed, we disarmed ours.

We thanked the farmer for all the extra stuff he gave us; there was a stack of stuff in this place. This officer came up to us we told him we had all these blasted charges he said "for Christ sake don't get hurt, or else they will have me". Unfortunately it was the other way round. We said we had these boxes of ammunition for these machine guns, I don't know what he wanted them for, we said, "help yourself take as many as you want".

So this is what happened to him, they drove back to where they were photographing Anzio before the breakout, we was on the other side of the Tigre, and unfortunately he trod on a mine and blew his leg off, and of course that was the last we saw of him. It just shows how dangerous these weapons were. The next officer we had was pretty good. In fact I can say this from the day we landed in Anzio I was able and fit soldier, in fact my discharge papers said I was an exemplary soldier.

Well anyway the farmer came over thanked us very well, we thanked him too and he said here you are and he gave us three sheep. Salted, skinned ready for cooking, this was just before we lost our officer. The last time he came up to us we said to him "the farmer gave us three sheep" he said "right I will take them back and we will have them" and I said "don't forget send us up some" he said "don't worry you have will the pick of it" which we did. The following day he came up and that was unfortunately the last time we saw him.

There was something else now he came up to us. We got back and we told the section that came up to relieve us the help that we received as we got some very good vino from the farmer and we told him that this lot was ok as some of this were from the 8th Army with us.

Letter home that Fred Sent

"Well dear heres a photo I had done in Rome and you can see my medal on this one. I'm OK give mum one and Charlie one from me. I hope you get the parcel OK dear. Well dear I don't look too bad considering there's a war on yours with all my love Fred"

Rome

Some of the Italians were involved in a massacre at some caves just outside Rome, and they were going on trial when a crowd attacked them, killed some and threw some into the river Tiber. We were told to keep out of it, which we did.

Whilst in Rome we did a lot of sight seeing and one particular trip I went to the Colosseum and I also carved my name in there. I carved my name in some tunnels at Gibraltar. Some of the lads got on top of the Colosseum and to try and take photos and fell off. I think at least two were killed doing this.

We had these tickets for our food. We went to these great big restaurants, and I have never tasted corned beef on how they done it up. I had three slices of this corned beef and potatoes. I think it was the most marvellous lunch I have ever had. Of course we did have a lot of wine, but as all good things come to an end, in the morning we were told to get all gear together. We got the trucks up and in went the gear and up we went. We went on then until the snows come down and we heard the bells of Bologna.

Everything was nice and still. That Christmas, and although I am jumping ahead, we heard the Germans singing in there dugouts or whatever and we got the mortars trained on them give them a few bursts and they did the same to us. That was the Christmas one.

After Rome

Anyway we went back and up we went to place called Salerto. I think we took over from an American division. On our left we had a Japanese division, these were Japanese lads who were born in America and were interred. They were allowed out if the sons joined up which they did and in front of us was a Russian division which they gave themselves up. We were getting supplied by the Italian partisans. We had Italians fighting with us, and they did a good job.

My mate Geordie ran in to a German hospital and there was some infantry, well they were frightened to go in case of booby traps. So Geordie went in and he came out with four bottles, and it must have been alcohol, do you want some of this he said, and I said no bloody fear. I will put that in some vino. Geordie he drank two bottles, then Jeep came up and said "Geordie dying". We went round and had a look at him. The doctor had a look at him and said "he is stupefied". So what we did we rolled him up in our blankets and put him in our truck. In the lorry there was explosives and different stuff. Two days later when we took him out

345

he had crapped and weed in his blankets, he stank the truck out and it was days before we got the smell out of the truck. He was still out and our sergeant he didn't know about him.

Letter from Iris

"To Fred, Happy Birthday darling and lets hope, please God, that we will be together for the next all our love dear Iris and Sonny Boy"

Florence

After our garrison in Rome we then moved forward, up to Florence. There was a big tank battle at Rimini and we went in there. It was virtually flat and people that have been out there now on holiday have told me that it has been built up back to normal, if you could get back to normal after that. After going round Rimini we went on to the final wotsname, which was Florence. This was where I got wounded. We stopped at Florence, we picked up our bits and pieces, we made ourselves into a fighting unit again and off we went. We went into Florence and we went to the bridge with houses on.

Florence had just been taken but we were having a breather from crossing the Arno. We used to go down to the Arno and we done the same as we did over the Sangro, bailey bridges which were under water, which was of course, something else different happened we had a floating bailey to put across. There was just enough water for it to float. I went to Desci, we blew this dam and this water trickled away, and the bailey settled down and broke on the bottom of the river. It was very deep in the middle and very shallow at the edges. It was also a little bridge across with the houses on, some pontoon bridge or other. I forget the name of that, and we went down to have a look at.

On the other side we could actually see the Germans but they were trying to make Florence some of its architectural beauties and open city. I think this thing banked and we rushed across. As Jerry's lobbed things in, anyway Italian partisans were coming into the picture, as I will explain later. The commander of the partisans used to talk to our people quite a lot, we knew the minefield across the other side, and we knew were the Germans were.

Then we went into Florence we paused to refit and then we went across. I found another thing here, when we took the bridge, and the Canadians then went straight through, the Canadian armoured. They then were carrying on towards I think the Gustav line. It was another big line the Germans had built up. Our main one was Pescara the Canadians then swept across and took Pescara with us.

Now this was this little episode, which happened on the outskirts of Florence. We moved into a big place and this was before I got done. I no I am moving around from one to the other one but this is just to let you know roughly where I am. I forget half the blasted names. We found a big house our troop went in there, we had all of our trucks with us still and we also had a load of rubber boats which we were going to take down to the harbour.

The Italian Partisans come up, these were the ones that were across the river some got killed, anyway they were telling us about tunnels, they weren't in the ground like we knew they were in the roofs of these big houses on the other side of the Arno river and it would appear they were hundreds and hundreds years old when they were like towns that were surrounded and being in charge like town governments.

The people in charge could listen to all the people that were talking and what they were doing and they were doing the same to the Germans. The Germans didn't know anything about it. I actually went up and saw one; this was before I was wounded. They had made their headquarters in one of these, the Germans had just left. They were finding food that the Germans had left behind and they said come up and see these tunnels. So up we went it and there it was, it was just wide enough for a person to walk along.

Anyway on the day we were to attack, we attacked, we rushed across. Partisans came down from the top. The Germans were just stunned the charges never went off. We then went with three partisans along the river bank and they showed us the minefield. The infantry that was coming across was the Beds and Herts, and they were attacking up the road to where the partisans told them where the Germans were the strongest. It must be the first major engagement of that regiment as they came from Malta to relieve our Guards brigade which was going home and then go to France. We then went along with these three partisans until we get to minefields. We started clearing the minefield. There were only seven of us including these three partisans and the four of our men.

Now this happened after the war, a mate of mine, at the record office, he got my company's war diary. He got the day I was wounded about what we were doing where we going and so on, burying mines, lifting them, and dealing with booby traps and so on. At the bottom of it, it said two soldiers were wounded by a booby trap and had to be evacuated. Now this is what really happened. We were lifting mines and there were three of us, and we were waiting for the Scots. We had cleared a partial lane for them to come through. We then went back to the river where the rest of our troop was bringing the Royal Scots across in boats. There was a tape they we had laid right down. We had come from the small bridge over the Arno that splits the two sides of Florence. We had cleared that and had gone right along the bank was to where this point was.

This is what they put in the war diary. They had casualties and two soldiers were wounded by blast. Never put down one was an Italian Partisan. If we had set the booby traps off we would have both been killed. We never did. They were very short on what happened. I have got this letter saying the day I was wounded; they can check this with the war diary. I have put a couple in from my war unit so they can see how they explained it that we were OR's. I used to hate the term OR. Other Ranks that means. On all the war diaries and I have 5 – three from 23rd Field Company and 2 – from 626 field squadron, it lists the number of people were killed and names the officers but not the names of the OR's. OR's were just OR's. I also listed the one on the day I was wounded, it stated on there that it was just after we got over the Arno river and we cleared the mines ready for the arrival for the Royal Scots. I didn't like that expression I was a sapper. A sapper was reasonable he was as a good as a private. I wouldn't have minded that.

Unfortunately at this time two other sappers – Jimmy Hardman and Young Joyce (he was the youngest sapper), were clearing the mines and a bunch of Italians refugees came along. The Germans used to leave them alone, as they caused the Allies more trouble than the Germans. So Jimmy Hardman went up to stop them and get them into single file, and to come over this crater. At the same time at the back of house were mines that were ready to put in. They were German tellermines. They were in stacks, four or five in a stack. They were going to put on the road or the ground of back gardens.

Suddenly we heard gun fire and that was unfortunately the Italian partisans getting killed. I suppose they gave as good as they got. The one with me and he shouted out, and there was 8 Germans walking along the road and they were coming along the cutting were my two mates were. Of course there were all these Italian refugees.

The next phrase was when I got wounded. The official explanation, which I have got, just says they were clearing the banks of the river – mines, the Italians were helping us. Two soldiers were wounded, that was an Italian Partisan and me. We were evacuated after much trouble, which it was. This is what happened - we were clearing this road there was Jimmy Hardman another nipper named Joyce, Jeep Middleton was down on the banks of the river because they were dragging these boats across with the Royal Scots.

The Italian that was in the house, because all of the houses were empty but before that Joyce and Jimmy Hardman signalled to me because you couldn't talk we didn't know where the jerry's were, and pointed up the road and there was a crowd of

353

Italians coming along there. There was a crater and some mines that hadn't been cleared which we weren't bothering with as we were trying to clear this lane, which these infantry the Royal Scots, were going to go up.

The Italian Partisan said to me from the doorway "Tedesco" which meant Germans and we both went into the house there wasn't a booby trap there. If there had been a booby trap there we would have been killed. We looked out and there was a string of Germans about ten or twelve going across the front.

I went back because I left my Sten gun outside; I got my Sten gun went back in. Looked through what was left of the window. The Italian Partisan only had a revolver. I tapped my gun and he knew what I meant. We opened up and went straight along the rank, two of them fell down, and the others didn't even lie down. They started firing at the house.

There was a line of Germans now coming across the field, there must have been eight or nine, and they were in single file. They were firing now at the partisans a covering party, I don't know what happened to the other ones, but this one was killed. We fired back so many Germans fell down and the others just grabbed them and started firing at the house where I was firing from.

Now outside this house was a heap of teller mines, all armed. That's the big anti tank mine. Of course they were firing bazookas at us, and these small schmizers. One bullet hit me; it came through the wall because I was hiding round behind the wall you see. It hit me in the bloody arm and as we went to run out so these bazookas must have hit the mines. They went up in the air and so did the bloody house and down it came on me. Underneath the rubble I could hear the fighting carry on. Anyway Jimmy Hardman had seen it, and Jimmy Hardman shouted and started digging me out.

As we went to run out of this house, it must have been a bazooka that hit one of these mines. I never heard any explosion but Jimmy Hardman said, "Christ the whole house went up and we thought you set off a booby trap". I suppose that is where the information came from on that piece of paper. When they got us out I couldn't remember how long I was in there. I must have been unconscious. The partisan was unconscious and was unconscious when they dug him out. After they dug us out they had to keep stopping as they were being attacked with mortars and lots of wire which made them think it was booby trapped. So they had to trace the wires before they could carry on digging again. Anyway we were dug out.

They got us both in the ambulance we got the infantry passed. We put in next to the driver; the Italian partisan was on a stretcher on the side. I tried to talk to him before he died, to try and find out if he was a catholic and did he need a priest. I didn't much care about myself in that regard.

Then we went down to the Arno. We went across the Arno. We got mortared going across the blasted Arno most of them went into the river anyway one of them could of hit us. We then went to Sienna and there was a big American transport plane, I was walking wounded but unfortunately they had found that this Italian Partisan that was with me was dead. I see them put him at the side of the airfield. I told the doctor that he had been with me 1st Infantry Division. He just wrote it down and said, "Alright I'll put it down as dead on arrival". By then you could see that there was some trouble on as you could see lines and lines of stretchers along with the walking wounded – Canadian, American and British. Anyway they didn't make any differential between us. As we came up, we went straight onto the plane and off to Naples.

I got into this plane and another funny thing was this very tiny nurse, she must have been the smallest person, even smaller than Iris. Very cheerfully she said "it wont be long you are going to see Naples, I hope you are not going to die". She was going round with little brown paper bags and she said "if any of you feel sick feel free to use these bags" and that was that. [Laughs]. The pilot took us right over Vesuvius we actually looked down into the crater. Well I did. When we got down the ambulances were waiting for us, the Americans went one way and we went the other way. We went to our place, which was just outside Naples, in a big general hospital. I forget the number of it now, a double figure number.

Just outside Naples was a British General Hospital, I then found out I had been shot in the arm and a piece of shrapnel in my head. There were a number of abrasions made by bits of stone. The nurse found the bit of shrapnel – she was scraping my face. My hair had been burnt off and all she had to do was rub her hands all over it and it all fell off. I think I had a number of abrasions – one, two, three, four, five, six, seven – I had seven. Unfortunately it later turned out that I had little marks on my face called rodent ulcers which the doctor in Portsmouth cut out. That happened along time afterwards. She found this little bit of metal it was only as big as my little fingernail. The colour of it was German; it was the German colour for their weapons. I carried that and the bullet which came through the house and belted me in the arm. Blood had come out onto the shirt and it had congealed in the shirt, and the bullet was in the shirt. So when she cut if off it fell out. When I looked at my arm there was a little dent. That was that. The piece of shrapnel and the bullet she gave me. She scrapped my face and my arm. I was in that hospital for about three weeks. I had a lot of trouble with eyes and ears. They gave me a pair of sunglasses to wear as the sun was warm.

As a result of the explosion I had a perforated right ear, shrapnel wounds to face and arms blast injury to face and eyes, as well as having nightmare disorders. These nightmare disorders about being buried alive continue to affect me to this day. The shrapnel and pieces of stone, which marked my face, have now developed into rodent ulcers. My head still buzzed and my ear was deaf and perforated, but I was glad when I got back to my unit.

When I applied for work abroad (when I returned home), I was rejected by the fleet medical officer because of my war disabilities that were caused during this attack.

When I returned to my unit my OC what had happened. After I told him he said, "every time I write in my diary that a Sapper is killed or wounded I write NO LIGHT WORK". In the war diary, which I later managed to get, this was what was put in the diary against the 3rd September 1944.

I suffered "blast injury to eyes" in 1944 and also I have been totally deaf in one ear since my injury. This is listed as "perforation right ear"

From the medical notes of Fred Britt

3rd September 1944

Field Ambulance diagnosis – mine wounds (booby trapped) of right arm. Condition good. Dressings removed.

14.00 hrs. Lacerations of forehead, superficial abrasions of right arm. Evacuate by air – hears noises in ear, result of blast injury.

4th September 1944

General hospital notes – mine wound, left arm and forehead (note not left but right arm!) Lacerations of forehead, superficial abrasions right arm, and buzzing in ears.

5th September 1944

2nd Degree burn right forearm – cleaned with flavine and dressed, leave for 5 days.

11th September 1944

Small intestinal haemorrhages. No treatment necessary except avoid water in ears.

15th September 1944. Areas healed. Transfer to con Depot. Condition on discharge – satisfactory.

8th October 1944 – convalescent depot. Date arrived 19th September 1944 from 69 Brigade General Hospital. 20th September 1944 – all wounds healed no disabilities.

7th October 1944 – discharged back to company.

My right arm is still painful. My hearing was impaired, and also I had nightmares of water running and rats

We loved collecting things and this applies to red devils. A little grenade the Italians used to throw at you, and there were hundreds of them around. We had a ready market as the Americans bought them all. we disarmed them and they used them for lighters. When I was wounded and departed back to the rear, Jimmy Hardman took my kit, which I had left at side of the road to the quartermaster. He nearly had a fit and nearly jumped through the roof when he opened my small pack because it was full of Italian Hand grenades which we used to call red devils. Most of them were disarmed and we used to flog these to our allies and friends.

My time in that hospital was pretty good but my time in a South African convalescent depot was out of this world, and no one had better talk to me about apartheid. They were excellent and I think apart from my time in the garrison of Rome, were my best time in the Army. After I got better I went to Capri and Naples General Hospital and finished up in a South African convalescent depot where we did all the wotsname up. Still aching and paining, I was deaf in one ear, as one ear drum was perforated. I still went back to the front and back to the wotsname and they were short of sappers and there were more booby traps. Anyway I survived.

It was different between like chalk and cheese from the British to the South African army. We got issued with clothes, all new brand new clothes, dumped all the rest. Then we done a very gentle physical training and then we had talks generally about South Africa. Then they got us ready for two days on the isle of Capri, in Gracie Fields villa. Where all we had to do was walk about and take in the scenery. Naples bay was horrible it was full of oil and sunken ships. We got on the other side though it wasn't too bad. After that we had another couple of trips to Salerno. We could then see the trouble that the lads got into when they landed there. There was a British infantry division with the Americans when they landed. The Hampshire's played a right big part in it. After that we went back to South African convalescent depot, unfortunately the next trip was to a British holding place ready for going back up the line. After that we did our very vigorous training. The way back was the most complicated one that I have ever done.

Anyway all good things come to an end. I then ended up in a re-enforcement unit in transit for about six weeks. As the unit about now was well up Italy, they kept screaming for men and eventually they did. There were about 28 sappers from our division, they got a truck and shoved us in it and up we went and joined them.

After being wounded

I finished up and had been wounded and was now ready to go back to my unit. This was a funny way they sent me back. We were taken to a transit camp, along side of it was a place where divisions came down with their trucks to get supplies and we were told to wait for our divisional trucks, get on and off we go. I found out the 4th Indian Division and the 78th British Infantry Division and our own which was the 4th Armoured Brigade were in the same area. So they said get onto any truck going up, and those divisions and that will take you into an echelon of that division or your brigade.

So we waited and the next day in came a convoy of trucks from the 4th Indian Division, we piled in like they said and off we went. The funny thing was it took us two days to get into our area, and the whole time we were living on japatis, they would stop off in different transit areas and get out their supplies and make their japatis and share them around. Of course we would come and have some.

We eventually we did get near our area and then we were waiting in this ammunition area. We waited for any trucks, or tanks, armoured carriers, or Bren carriers or transport to the 4th armoured brigade which eventually came. This was three of us for the 4th Armoured Brigade. Eventually in came a white's car from our own unit.

We just went over to him and said "Right we have got to go back", so he said "We mainly come down to get malaria drugs – mepropane, soon as we get you can you and your kit aboard and we can get back". We arrived back in our own land more or less. We talked about what happened and how we got done. The other two lads, were not in my company but were in the same squadron in different troops, had got first wounded when we first took the Arno. They were on a bridge that got hit.

We were now back with our unit, after three or four days, I told everybody what had happened and they said "A well one story is good as another" and off we went. My first job when I come back, I already talked about it when we were going up this road and there was a line of German trucks that we found but the first one had blown the wheel off on their own mines.

Mine clearing after Florence

Now I think the next phrase was the gothic line. We went forward, we were clearing mines. The Germans used to leave big areas unoccupied, they just to leave it to the mines. They used to hold the high ground, they pretty much had it all taped off.

We went forward one day to clear mines, as one of our infantry units was had a troop carrier, the driver and one other was killed, and two of the crew were killed. So the commander sent us up, we swept the area, we found quite a few of these teller mines and a new mine which had just come out as far as we were concerned. It was of Italian manufacture and it was a long wooden mine. We found a few of these on the verge. On the side of the road was a minefield which I had never seen before and I was tempted to set fire to it, but you do things like that and you have to have authority. They were stakes with a hand grenade surrounded by concrete that was lashed to the post. As you know or should know, a German hand grenade had a long piece of wood which gave them an extra long throwing power. Up through this wood on this stake was a piece of cord which was partially pulled out, not fully pulled out. Then tied on the opposite, so you had two grenades with a wire between it if you struck that – boom, boom, that's what would have happened.

We found a long road and a German wagon which had hit its own mine. We didn't put mines down there we were taking them out. The wheel had blown off and the driver was hanging out the truck. There were loads of flies hanging around so he must have been dead for some time. The wagon – a diesel wagon, had loads of tins of that cabbage stuff they used to eat – Saur kraut. They were saying "watch out, it might be booby trapped – remember Fred you just come back". I got some of the stuff and it wasn't too bad. He had a pipe which had come out of his pocket and fallen on the floor. I took that as a souvenir.

When they tried to get away the first truck struck a mine, and there was a lot of blast. The door was off and also a driver was dead. What we didn't know there was an Italian Police station, which we found out later. We were sent back to destroy the mines. There were only the same men when this happened. What we done, was they were teller mines, not schue mines which are in the ground. The teller mines we emptied as some of that we could use for fires. You could burn it. We were emptying these out, and a path that led off to what we thought was farms was a village – San de mer something, I can't remember the name.

Anyway then four or five Italians and three or four partisans came along. I had been wounded with a partisan and unfortunately he died. These had a handkerchief with a symbol in of the area and a letter stating where they came from. These partisans had the same neckerchief as what the one that was killed. I told them this in my perfect Italiano. They said "They didn't know him but that was the area" they were mostly ex-soldiers and police. Anyway the place what I was describing as a police place was being used by the Germans as a front line for injuries.

In fact there were two dead Germans in there. We got the two Germans out; these partisans said "Could we let them have the gear that was in there?" It was ammunition; I took the some of the smaller stuff which I could use. We took some of the ammunition, but the tins of food; I think it was cabbage, not much meat. The Italians took it all and they were very grateful. I used to collect things and suddenly some of the notes which were banned by the British, and I had some of them. In fact I brought some of them home. I am not sure what they did on the other side, they cleared it all out. The two trucks that was reasonable, they took bits and pieces off it, and took it into this place. I said "all they are going to do is put the Italian flag up and paint it on these trucks, as we wouldn't use them". I said "I was a collector of different things", I got some Italian badges which I was very please with, and they were as well.

Then I heard a big bang. We saw some American officers, and there were three of them. What had happened and they had come up on our right and were looking for a place to park cars, their divisional transport, and there was a jeep near to them. We saw they were in the middle of a bloody mine field, we shouted "Stay still"; we went along where it was already swept.

You could see where they went into the mine field, but the mine field wasn't recognised mines they were hand grenades, and they were German hand grenades on long sticks, with a string you pulled out like these poppers you use now for these gala nights in the clubs and that. They were either tied together or tied on a stick, and nearly pulled out, so all you had to do if your foot kicked one especially as there was something growing over it. Anyway we got into where we could get hold of them and let them out. There were two of them and one wounded.

Unfortunately by the time we got he out he was calling for his mother. He was dead. We got them out and back to their jeep and they were shook up. They said "thank you very much" and took our unit and that was all we heard from them. We then went back to our unit and carried on. You could see where our unit was, there was all clouds and bangs going on. Eventually we got up to where there were a number of our tanks. By now we had cleared and filled in all the craters and the road was more or less you could go up it.

We did set fire to this ground, it burnt straight through and some of the mines did go off. You could see them a bit better after this. As most of them were just above the ground, you couldn't see them properly. The officers who went into a mine field, this is something no one should do. It was alright for us, we were trained for this of work but you would go for a shite and you would go for a shite. It was an expression.

After this we went to a place called San Veto, but before this we did a little diversion to a river. The old man said "we have some landing craft here and there was a ford further up, so we will put some of our armour across". So some sappers went across there but I went on the boats with some Bren carriers and we did a small diversion round. We caught the Germans with their trousers down, literally. When we went back to a dump for food, Tommy Trinder the comedian was holding a get together on the steps of a church. He was a very funny fellow and before we knew where we were two hours had gone by. There was a load of us there, Canadians and British.

ENSA was the troop that looked after our artistic things, and the number one man was Tommy Trinder. I don't know if you have heard of him. Of course eventually our old man came up and went "Come on, you got do this and that", we got to our unit which was further along to the proper place as the Germans couldn't blow the bridge now, as we came up behind them too quick.

Italy minefield – after Florence

We got a few souvenirs and we re-joined our unit. We were moving along to the next battle, a few days afterwards. We took some explosives back that we found in teller mines and we used to use them start a fire when we wanted to brew up. There were no detonators so they wouldn't go bang. The teller mines was easy to dispose of schue mines were harder. So where the mines we had sandbags and a long piece of wire that we used to use for telephones and we used to drag it over it. You had to do it very quick and it would fire the mine. Anyway as we cleared up that area a bit.

We went into a big house, and the grounds, we put our bivets up. We were waiting for our sapper gear to come up; it was quite a flat area with no rivers. The big house, there was a man who was looking after it and an American Officer. He was taken a reference of the house. He said "these people have helped the allied cause and I he would have liked that no one would use the house", which was a bit funny because just after he said that, a couple of Messerschmitts came shooting up the road, shooting through it and through his jeep. Our old man said "look if there is anyone going to be safe in that house they can't go in the house". I can't blame him for that. One of our jeeps took him back and then the Americans came along took the damaged jeep back.

There was a big castle, not quite but it was a house. There were Italians in there, and we did eventually go in there and there were three or four more Messerschmitts came by and they have a go at our bivets. So we moved them to under the trees and dispersed our trucks just in case, as we had quite a bit of transport, mostly white's cars. We were there for about a fortnight and the owner then came back from Florence. This American officer was with him so they must have known and told never to go in the place. Eventually we were moved on and rejoined the division.

We came under our old friend – shellfire so we knew we were near the front. Our lot going in, and the 3rd division coming out, we knew then we were going to have another go at the Hun.

Tito

There was a lot of activity and some Royal Marine Commando's had come across from Yugoslavia. On a clear day you should have been able to see it, but it was too bloody misty. They opened up a big area to bring the partisans in. Of course by now most of unit especially the infantry had gone forward. Possibly the next big battle was going to be on the Sangro. Anyway we cleared this area and these partisans came in and they looked a right shower. They had showers and new clothes which we supplied, and they looked a reasonable bunch.

There was a buzz that I have said this before that was working at Leigh Park when I had an over in Riders lane, his name was Doctor Rickards. He was our medical officer, we saw him buzzing around and then a lot of our infantry went across the Adriatic. What happened was the Germans didn't know this; they had shot and wounded Tito. They had him in a fort in Yugoslavia and they were going to shoot him. Anyway our raiding party got him out and brought him back. Doctor Rickards was the one who took the bullets out. I met him as I could remember him, when he used to shoot pigeons with a dentist in Riders Lane in Leigh Park. I said about I was in the 4th Armoured Brigade and "Yes" he said "these pigeons bothering you?" and I said "yes". Every anniversary of Tito they used to invite Doctor Rickards back to Yugoslav before he died. I think he is dead now as well.

After that little episode, the partisans, of course, used to get all their uniforms and food and god knows what and back they used to go to Yugoslavia to cause mayhem, which they did, to the Germans. The Germans didn't like being anywhere near them. We now came into more contact with the Italian partisans; of course the Italian Partisan army was more into the centre of Italy. They were now coming over and telling us about different things, of course we were spreading out.

Italy – Last battles

On the way there to Trigno, we landed at San Vito and we went to the beaches to San Vito we had got over a river and it was quite a simple. As soon as we came ashore and the Germans and we came over the back of the Germans, the Germans never knew the size of the landing party was it wasn't very big was a couple of tanks and a squadron of sappers two companies of infantry. We had armed bulldozers and we had a carrier that destroyed mortar placements. I used to think that if it did explode in the tank to use the old Churchill. We only carried two.

Up comes your armour and away goes your track. As used to come back then to sweep around. I got my units daily movements on what we did and some of them you could read that after they have moved around the tanks so we could move.

This little episode happened in Italy and concerns the Americans. We got on very well with the Americans especially the coloured ones. They would drive most of our Lorries in Anzio and up to the fixed lines when we were fighting in the gothic line. They would loan their equipment at the drop of the hat. You only had to say you need so and so and it was there. This little episode gave us a taste of rations. We used to have mostly American rations and our compo but our compo was much better. I said this episode was in Italy and it was in the Gothic line.

Naples

I have got most of unit's war diary, now this happened in Naples. Now I don't know if everyone knows there were two important places, there was the house where the American gangster was born and there was the palace where Nelson met Lady Hamilton. We went to both of them because the palace was where Nelson and Lady Hamilton met had been taken over by the NAAFI and we used to have our tea and cakes there when we were having a look round at the sights. The other one was Vesuvius when I was brought down from the front I was in an American Dakota I had come down from Sienna, and there was a little tiny nurse and it was better than our Dakotas that we used to go in. First thing as we got into the plane she gave us a brown paper bag to be sick in.

The pilot was very cheerful, he said, "There was an old saying about see Naples and die but I going to fly over Vesuvius" as the landing place was very near there. He did and we had a look down at the volcano and then he landed and I went into the British Hospital.

Italy

As we approached winter we were slowing down. We were digging the road right round the side of a mountain. As the approaches of the mountain were under observation of the Germans, this was towards Bolerno. It was called the Sunset Trail we built it in two weeks, toiling up steep gradients and appalling weather, frost and snow. Our HQ or our billet was an old church, and in the church was a donkey, it was a sort of pet. He used to eat everything we had – mostly biscuits. On our left was a division of American Negros and they were very useful to us. As we put minefields down and extended along their front, they gave covering fire for us.

Little Donkey

This little episode in Italy and it happened before the meat fiasco in Italy. We used to have a donkey which hung out when we were billeted in a church. This donkey used to roam outside and unfortunately we didn't know anything about this to afterwards. Germans mortared the position and the donkey was killed. The poor little donkey got some shrapnel; anyway they shot it. The cooks skinned and cut the donkey up, (we didn't know anything about this) and they made a smashing great stew out of this poor old donkey. Well young donkey.

We were rather surprised, we came back off this road, and it was called the Sunset Trail. They dished out great big bits of stew that they had, it lasted two or three days this stew did, bit different from our own rations. Later we learnt it was a poor old donkey that they had cut up.

Stealing meat from the Americans

Anyway one night we watched a couple of houses further down in the valley in their zut zuts, you couldn't miss them with their brown faces against the snow, stuck out like no ones business, and we could watch them. We were more or less a bit camouflaged. We saw them carting whole beef sides where their cookhouse was a bit further along. The cookhouse was into the side of a big hill. They used to slice up and eat it, I should imagine. One day Jeep came to me and he said "Oi we should get some of that meat", and he said" if you watch from this road here you can see that this sentry walks round and you can time him"

We saw the American sentry coming round and as he passed as there was no door, we went straight in. We carried a spare zut-zut, and we were both dressed in white. We put it on the carcass of beef and I managed to get in my shoulder. Jeep watched my back which meant that the sentry was now on his way back and out we went. We had to climb a small hill onto the road and across the road where we were billeted. I think it was Mount Blanc I was climbing;

anyway we got up and over. Got it into the church and it was frozen solid. Our cook come over "what the bloody hell have you got there?" he said. As most of our rations were biscuit and corned beef. He said "When it thaws out we will cook it". It took over a day to thaw out and we had two great big slices. I think the old man was going to give us the MM (Military Medal).

Safe cracking in Italy

We are now going very fast through Italy and we were in Lake Como area. Now the Germans had taken up position in the heights in high ground. In normal circumstances they would have mined down on the lower roads so that if their artillery if they heard anything could play havoc with you. We would have gone out in night and checked them out to see what mines they were using. They were using none. All the roads leading north were completely clear. So when we went back and reported everyone started to get on the alert and partisans that had accompanied us up from Florence said "There are a lot of strange partisans from the north down here". We found out why in a few days later, through our glasses we saw a very big convoy of trucks that had come through over or around the lake. Then they had stopped because what we had done was each infantry man used to carry a Hawkins grenade we tied these onto telephone wires and pulled them across the roads. So nearly every road in that area had these mines on our side. We used to carry them on the middle of our bags on our webbing.

We then saw quite a lot of partisans and we told not to interfere. When they lined up to what we took to be German soldiers and some of our fellows went forward with some of our officers and had an argument with them and we got them away. It was rather silly as if they had shot them then the Germans would have seen this. We were watching most of this through glasses so it was obvious that the Germans were. We could see a German truck that had been hit by a mine by one of these mines that we pulled across. It was followed by a long convoy. The partisans from the north, that seemed to be in charge marched off or took the wagons over and went off. We later learnt that they were the Italian government that was trying to get out including Mussolini. According to partisans they hadn't got far until they were all marched into a barn and they were all shot. I think this was 4 or 5 days later we went into one of the big Italian cities Milan to get some food rations. We saw all the Italians including Mussolini mistresses hanging up on street lights and the Italians were spitting at them. For a civilised country it was rather strange.

Several of us were sent into the city as our brigade was resting round about Lake Como and we had to go into Geneva and the old man said "take some explosives we think the CMB's have a safe they want opening". So we took a lot of our stuff a lot of explosives and some stuff we got out of German mines. They had little round sticks of explosives with a detonator you screwed on we used these or own detonators.

We got there and we had to go to the divisional CMP. When we went in there and we saw the fellow in charge and said "there are two big safes" He took us down and they were reasonable safes and we had to drill out where the tumblers were so we could put explosives in. We used to have a detonator pencils, we would poke that in turn it up for a time and that exploded. So we cleared and the only thing I was a bit winded about if they had put an explosive charge inside the safe so when we fired that fired but actually it didn't. When we did open it and we had to use several detonators before we did and we found inside unfortunately I think the MP's knew what was in there as they stopped with us even when we said "there could be a booby trap in here". We got a way and they reluctantly left and it was possessions of our entire merchant seaman that had been caught money watches and things like that, it had been taken and put in this safe. Unfortunately the Camp's were watching us, and we didn't fancy taken stuff that belonged to some of the men, as they might have been killed.

Last Battle in Italy

Further back onto this road Jerry used to sometimes mortar just above it. This was going along side of the mountain than stuff would come down and smash our little road. We had to go up there at night mostly and on this ledge of tree trunks and put the road back on top of it again. It was only used by mules. Further round out of view of the enemy was a stretch road which we controlled by telephone. IF anything was coming out they used to phone the red caps on the far end and he would stop traffic coming. There was a big area that backed on to It.

One day we had gone up and we were bringing back some explosives on the mules. We got to the going up and then coming out was a mule train, there was some Italians and they were bringing some dead out. Unfortunately there was a flurry of snow and a few mortars which never came anywhere near us. We started off when we found it was clear and halfway through; there was a drop below, a real drop we then more or less came face to face. We had three mules and they had about four. There was a bit of trouble going on. Even the mules knew something was going on. So the mules got shot that were carrying the dead and they had to go over the side. Our section with the explosives on went forward. We had to take the Italian Muletineers with us until we got to a safe position and they could pass. They were down there for a few days; you could see them down there.

We kept getting bursts of snow and you could hear the bells of Bologna from where we where. I saw my wives uncle; he was at a big ration centre which was down by the river. We used to go down to that and it was real feat to get back up the road. Charlie Tutton of a Portsmouth company of the Royal Engineers I saw him and said "What you doing here?" This was the second time I saw him, I saw him the western desert of Africa as well. I forget what division he was in.

Anyway we now went on and I am going to explain now my last battle when we got to up to the far of Italy as far as we could get. We were in now we were facing Germans, at the border of Austria. The 1st Infantry Division had gone as far up Italy as we could go. We were getting ready to go into Austria, and there were some going off sideways to Yugoslavia or Albania. One night after we had a talk about what we were going to do the following day, 7 sappers, including myself were told to go and report to the 1st company of British troops that was as far up as they could go.

It appeared that even when the Germans should have been at there lowest they were still coming through between the 1st infantry division and this American Division. Once they go through then they used to raise havoc before they went back. Once the firing started everyone got down, but the Germans they went back

Anyway this is main bit we had cut a trail in the side of a mountain, and it was called the sunset trail. One side as we were still in the 5th army was an American division, our division and an Italian division but as we went towards the city of Bologna, you could hear the bells in the churches. Anyway there were two sorts of sides, on the same mountain range, but German fighting troops used to get through, recce patrols and fighting patrols. They decided they want a string of mines unfortunately they were American mines.

This is about mines, mostly anyway. Mines played a big part of our job as sappers; no doubt they played a big part in saving our men's lives and positions from being over run. This one was our last one in Italy before we were taken out and then to be sent into Europe. The division had stopped getting ready to go into Europe proper.

We were waiting first of all to clear a river and second of all for some more transport to come up. We sent for by the infantry, the British Infantry, holding the line. Anyway there was a gap between and they were worried about even if the Germans were retreating they could come down the gap and shoot up ammo at the back of us. So to stop it we were to put a minefield between the American Division and our own division. There were only 21 mines but they were American mines – jumping jacks. This was a very covered valley and as things were heating up.

The Americans brought us the mines and we put them in. It was the first time I had used these. The mines, the jumping jacks, as everyone knows to fire it jumps up in the air, and away it went ball bearings everywhere. It was very similar to an S mine the Germans had. As I said they were American, you had to take out of pin with a screw in. It was armed once you had covered it up.

We had no NCO, I was the senior sapper, we then went up and saw the sergeant in charge of the infantry and he also pulled an officer, I think, from the Royal fusiliers and an officer from the American division. They then decided on putting in an arc of these mines.

Our sergeant said, "Oi Britt you are the one that does the booby traps, go on take seven men with you". So I took my troops, my company I wont say troops. We weren't in an Armoured Brigade then we were in an infantry brigade. Anyway we goes up as I said, with bags of stuff from the Americans and of course these blasted mines. I hated putting these jumping jacks in. I didn't mind the other ones, as they were for tanks, these were for men. We dug the hole out actually we had to wear suit suits, they were a white camouflage suits because of the snow.

Anyway we dug, I think we put 21 in, in a very straight line or down and up on this connection. The Germans or the recce sections used to come through. Of course once they got through they could get anywhere. They had to get back but if they set off these jumping jacks then they were going to have a very hot reception. Which they did later on as we found out, but with the snow the boot of a British soldier and the boot of an American soldier and the boot of a German soldier all made different foot prints. Sometimes you could see the footprints in the snow and you could say that was so and so, that's so and so, that's British.

We put the 21 mines in, starting from just in front the American division, down to the river and up to the British machine guns were. As we took the pins out so, normally in our mines we used to give the pins to whoever was making the minefield map. In this case we gave them to a sergeant of the Americans. The mines were from them anyway; he did make a rough sketch of where they were.

The following morning we had to walk to a point on the mountain trail, we then had to walk to a point where we had our jeep to pick us up, to take us back to where we were staying, to where we were billeted, which was not very far back.

After this of course we wondering about if we were going to leave them, but when I see our sergeant. He came from Portsmouth, Cottle and the only thing I can see that he done anything good for me was when he dug us out when I got wounded back at Florence. The other thing was this, when we did go forward we never picked the mines up. We usually did if it is anything to do with our section. We found out from Sergeant Cottle that the Americans were going to lift them. And so we went off.

The next time I put something in was when we very nearly going into Europe. For about 4 or 5 days we had stopped and we put rockets in, which you just stuck in the ground, these were quite simple. A wire went from one to another and any that touched the wires; they shot up in the air like a warning pistol. We put about 7 or 8 in that was our last brush or nearly brush with the Germans because two days after that a battalion division came up and relieved us and we went back to the other side of Bologna.

We now seemed that the war in Italy was drawing to an end. Small units of our division were now heading towards the Poe valley. A lot of our units were going forward – the Canadians were trying to beat the Italian Partisans that were heading towards Yugoslavia. I think the Yugoslav Partisans were trying to take Trieste and other towns which they claimed was theirs. And so it seemed that the Allies were now starting to fall out.

Another thing that came into my mind, and he was a good friend and a Pompey fellow too, he was the last man to be killed on one of the rivers we were crossing. The bridge seemed to be intact, he was in the old squadron, and a dinko was running across the bridge when it exploded. He was blown to pieces with the officer in the dingo car. We made the crossing alright because of the Italians and Austrians showed us the way across. Then we went forward and the Germans had disappeared loads as prisoners but none as fighting units. All we were thinking about was going home – some thought!

"*2nd May 1945 Special Order of the day.*

Soldiers, sailors, airmen of the allied forces in the med theatre

2 years of fighting from the summer 1943 – invasion of Sicily – victors of the Italian campaign.

My admiration is unbounded and only equalled by the pride which is mine in being your commander in chief HR Alexander Field Marshall Supreme Allied Cdr Med theatre."

Then we were just repairing roads and moving anti aircraft missiles that had been dropped. When suddenly we were all told to get back to our billets, the company commander was going to give us a talk. The talk was like this he said, "I don't know where we are going we have been relieved and we are to go back to the last of the towns", I think it was Bologna, "and get re-equipped, de-loused and clean clothes and showers, that's all I can tell you at the time, so moving out first thing tomorrow morning".

Wilson Road, Portsmouth VE Day

We were prepared to go down towards Florence. Well most of our clothing which was lousy smelt, but you couldn't smell it until you got away from it. The next day we were given cans of petrol we have to go up and dump these clothes.

We handed all our kit in, stripped off, got cleaned up, got rid of the lice, got our hairs cut and a funny thing happened. There were a heap of under clothing that had been dumped it moved and we had to pour petrol over it and set fire to it. This Old Italian jumped up and said in broken English a lot of them could speak English. A lot of them had worked in America before coming back home. He said "Don't burn it, I'll burn it". He gave us a few presents and we went back to our camp, we had soaked it in petrol and don't know what he did with them, might have ate them.

Now just after this came the report that we were to move out and down the line. First of all we thought we had our gut full we must be going home, but this wasn't so. I will tell that later.

We then back, got all our clothes packed up, had our rough sleep and waited for the lorries to pick us up. We got emergency rations, which we were carrying. We went down on the lorries to just outside Bologna. There we went into a camp, got cleaned up, got showered, got all our hair cut off, got deloused, clean clothes, new uniform, all we kept was our webbing and our rifles. When then got into the different camps, and got laid up. We stayed another two days there. Meanwhile the division that relieved us, I think it was an Indian division, moved into Austria and into Europe. Of course the war was nearly over. We were put on to Lorries, and transported down toward Florence.

In our new billets we started repacking and getting new kit, especially tropical kit. Before we knew where we were, we were bound for Taranto. Anyway the following night we got into our lorries, they always travelled at night because of the luftwafte. There was no luftwafte this time we drove down south and there we dropped all our lorries and went onto a transit camp near a railway. We then put on the train, in these cattle trucks. We went down to Rome, in Rome we got out. We went to somewhere where we garrisoned in Rome. We went back through all of the battle areas, Rome, Naples, right down to Taranto. We were still as far as we were concerned in the 5th Army because when we stopped there were 5th Army snowdrops – we called them, like red caps with white on them. Anyway we waited for a train, which took us to Foggia then got out as Foggia had been very badly damaged. We went to a transit camp, which was now British.

Right through Italy there was a railway line. This was only went into operation just before Naples and after Naples and up towards Switzerland and Austria. Every so often a machine called a crusher used to (this was the Germans of course) shoots out the side and little charges used to drop on the line and every 20 foot there was a left and right and there was gap blown in the lines. Our railway engineers had to put in more or less new lines from Naples all the way up to Switzerland and Austria, to where we met the Germans. In fact we had to pull back down as we were under this agreement now, otherwise it was plain sailing.

Envelope of letter sent by Fred in 1945

Another day there and then we moved down to Taranto. Well this little episode happened at Taranto, there was a huge transit camp and this was before we went on the boat to the Middle East. All the way down the lads were jumping off all their collectable gear were flogging or turning it into army postal orders to send home, you used to have produce your pay book and they stamped it, how much you were handing in to change. Again you were only allowed to change so much when you got to Taranto, and I did want to say about poor old Jimmy Hardman. He went to do a crap hanging on the bar and I don't know what happened but the bloody bar and Jimmy went out the train, this was on the way down. We had the sense to sling his great coat out; he had his battle dress on or round his legs. To make sure he had his paperwork with him. Anyway he caught us up. The red caps picked him up [laughs], he told them what happened and they said, "Right you are very honest looking", he was civil engineer and was pretty good.

Anyway this concerned a division that came in from the Middle East from Afghanistan, it was an Indian division. Anything that the lads couldn't take, the money, they put down the toilet, the toilets were big holes and you sat on a pole and the smell that came up as over night when the Indians heard how much money was down there, they were down there. That's all you could hear slip, slop, slip, slop, taking these notes out, washing them, and hanging them out to dry. They were British military currency, American gold dollars, which couldn't be used there, and the lower ones of Lire, as I said at one time I was a millionaire when I collected all that stuff up and that's at the bottom of the drink. Those Indians thought all their birthdays had come; they had never seen so much money in all their life I shouldn't think. As I say you could only change so much, British military money wasn't too bad but American and Italian were rubbish as far as being able to spend it.

We were still unaware of where we were going. Then we saw this bloody great liner – the Duchess of Richmond, she was going to take us not to the UK but back to North Africa, or that's what we were told. When we were in this transit camp at Taranto, we got some extra money from gambling and wotnot.

Middle East

I thought probably there was too much damage was done in the channel ports and we were going back through the Mediterranean. We went back through the Mediterranean alright, there was the transports it wasn't landing craft it was liners. We were going back not to Blighty but to the Middle East. We first went to where there was a little trouble going on in Greece, just a few units especially around the islands.

After our initial work we were not to let the Greek Communists take over the weapons of the Germans, but we were to keep them armed until we got them back to the boats on the way back to the UK. No weapon was to be left in the hands of the communists. This was in Greece. The Sacred Brigade which had come from Italy, that was a different kettle of fish, they were very Greek Nationalists. We handed over to them.

We were now back in the Middle East. By this time the Corps commander had been changed and was still attached to the American army.

We ended up somewhere between Adeira and Beirut, and landed at Haifa where we were re-equipped, and were joined by volunteers from the Royal Navy, RAF regiment, and a detachment of army personnel from UK. It was pretty dark; there were all these army camps ready for us. We were sworn to secrecy, weren't allowed to tell our people where we were. The Germans had been beaten, and I think we thought what the bloody hell do they want us here for? Our trip down through Italy was conducted in great secrecy, as was our arrival in the Middle East. Instead of returning to the UK, we heard something very nasty, we were going to fight the Japanese.

Well I don't think that went down very well, we started training, and then we were being made up with draughts, first of all from the UK and draughts from the Royal Navy. They were coming from the Navy into the Army. There were also companies of the RAF regiment getting broken up and put into different companies within our division, the 1st Infantry division. Then we went on and we went on until we got to Damascus.

Preparation for Invasion of Japan

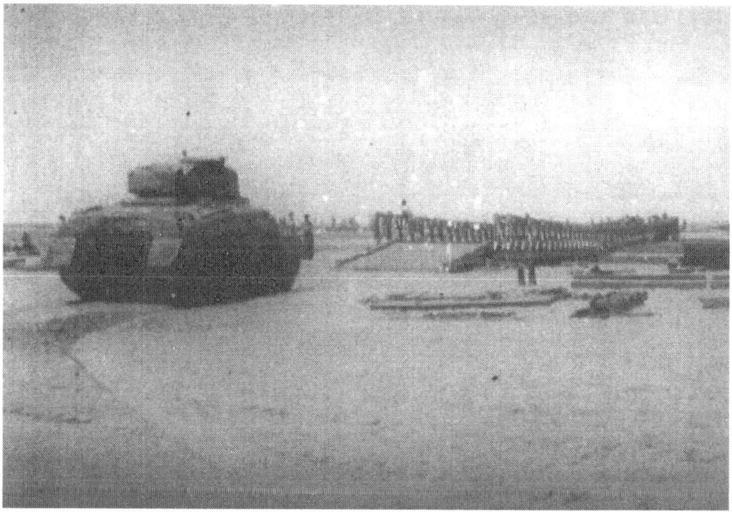

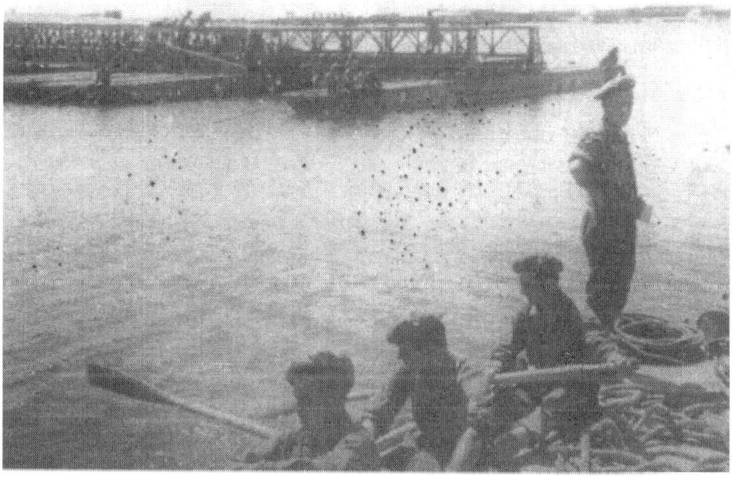

We had been re-equipped and we were getting ready to go Australia from the Middle East and we would have eventually ended up in Japan and they talked about how many casualties and what you had to do, and if you became a casualty. During one of inaugurations to Japanese the Adjuc came in with a signal saying a bomb had been dropped.

By the time we had done all our sea going bailey bridging, pontoon bridging, in the great lakes, we were ready for whatever we going to do. Then one day down come the adjuc and said "I'm sorry lads, but something has happened a bomb has been dropped or Hiroshima and Nagasaki, and it appears they wont want us in Japan, because Japan has packed it in." All the troops cheered until they nearly dropped because they knew they would not have to fight the Japs. They didn't realize at the time that there could have been fallout from those two atom bombs. So we thought, Christ they can't stop us going home now but they certainly did.

The 9th of August was my birthday, so we never did go to Japan and it the left the 1st Infantry Division free to answer the call to combat terrorism in the Middle East, in such places as Iran, Syria, Lebanon, Cyprus, Egypt and Palestine.

During this time, the Americans dropped the two bombs on Japan, and although these bombs were dropped a long way from where we were they were dirty bombs, and the fallout could have affected the Middle East. If this was the case, then as Japan had not ceased hostilities at the time, the results of this fallout could be deemed to be classed as, friendly fire.

When the Japanese war finished and we had to stand down our brigade, and the Free French brigade, as the French were still after taking control of Syria and Lebanon, as they did before. It turned out wrong; Britain and America guaranteed their freedom from colonial rule, a lot of good that done them. We used to roam around Persia, Iran, Iraq, Syria and all other places and finally collected up in Beirut. Before the fight between the French and the Syrians and we had to get in between. The French Foreign legion brigade which was with our lot went home, we didn't we went to Palestine until they decided that America was going to dominate the agreement, and although we were trying to keep the two sides apart we were sort of equal status. Eventually the Israelis took over; I don't think they will ever sort it out its worse than Ireland.

VJ Day – Wilson Road, Portsmouth

In 2001 I was treated for skin cancer on the left ear and the bridge of my nose. So was this the result of Fallout or the sun? Now if the fallout from the Japanese bombs did not cause that, as I have from good authority that the fallout dispersed in the Pacific. So the next thing is before the invasion of Iraq, the Iraq government buried the weapons of mass destruction in the mountains of Turkey,

Iraq or Iran. With the heavy rain and the breakage of the file, the rivers of Iraq became polluted with the fallout. Women and children caught and died of leukaemia. This is the only way I could have go skin cancer if the fallout from Japan did not touch Arabia.

When I was a gunner before I became an Engineer, and before the outbreak of the war, I was stationed on No Mans fort in the Solent. Although we off loaded food and ammunition, we never unloaded water. Where did it come from? This chap showed us the well, where the water came from. It came from Spain. So the water you are washing and bathing in came from Spain. When there was a heavy rainfall in Spain the water had to be capped. They used condense fluid to trace it from Spain.

When they dropped that bomb it changed the whole situation. After a few weeks of training we then went to Beirut, from Beirut we formed the Mobile Striking Force, which consists of a brigade from our division, two units from the French Foreign Legion and an Australian Battalion. Our job was to make sure that everyone kept the peace in places like Persia (now Iran), Iraq,

Syria, Lebanon and of course Jordan and Palestine. We were more or less continuously on the move. We ran around all these places as soon as something flared up. We then went where the trouble was then, which was of course Palestine. We were on prowl for the best part of my time in the Middle East. Eventually we went down for a rest first of all to the desert in Egypt – Sinai, and then right across Palestine in Beirut. That was one of the most beautiful cities I have been in and to see what it is like now, is unbelievable.

With the end of the war they gave us two weeks back pay, we got sent to Beirut and to a YMCA and put on buses. We went to Beirut and then onto the Golden Heights and into Damascus. It was another thing that happened there. In the celebrations of the square there, there was allsorts there, Americans, British, Australians, Arabs and all celebrating the end of was in Japan, after we bombed them. Anyway somebody slung a German flag down into the square there and blimey I thought it was about riots nothing like it. It was a German Nazi flag. They were tearing it to pieces. The red caps from about

15 different nations come in. eventually it quietened down and we went from Damascus to Jordan, and over the Allanbury Bridge and into Beirut.

We were told not to tell our people or write to them as our letters were still censored, to tell them where we were. So that in its self said we were going to go somewhere but our first day out me and four or five of my mates went to the church of the Holy Scpulchrc.

The Holy Sepulchre

Certificate of Pilgrimage.

The undersigned, the Very Reverend Archimandrite Kyriakos, Guardian and Superior of the Church of the Holy Sepulchre, hereby certifies that

Fredrich F. C. Britt

has duly visited the Church of the Holy Sepulchre of our Lord and Saviour Jesus Christ and the other Holy Shrines within the Basilica of the Holy Sepulchre and as a Pilgrim has made therein his pious devotions on this the 14 day of February in the year of Our Lord 1945 ; Whereof this Certificate signed and sealed in the Holy City of Jerusalem is a Witness.

We pray and beseech the Almighty and Eternal God that He will bless and save this Pilgrim, and will preserve him from all evil and danger.

Signed *Archimandrite Kyriaky*

Guardian of the Church of the Holy Sepulchre

We walked on the road that Jesus Christ walked with the cross. As we came to the YMCA and they took us into where we had some tea, but just near there was a photographer shop. In the window there were all the photographs of soldiers, American and British, and at the bottom of the photograph were the word Jerusalem and the name of the photographer. So I said, "Right we are going to get our photographs done". Me, Jimmy and Jeep went in there, and we had our photographs done separately. When we came out I put the photograph in a bible I had purchased. We had to go to the King David hotel (before it was blown up by terrorists) and we took them into a room there and there was an officer who was an Australian. He looked at the books and scribbled a note saying fine and everything. It was parcelled up and off it went and it arrived back home. I sent this parcel and Iris found out that I was in Jerusalem by this little logo. Some time later I got a letter from Iris saying I see you are in Jerusalem, "Oh" I said

In Palestine

We were the original ones from Africa and they talk about the forgotten armies. We were in pretty good condition and then everything in the Middle East started blowing up – Persia which is now Iran, Syria, Lebanon and of course Palestine. We found we were back in the thick of it and I looked forward to coming home. The elimination of Japan meant that the three divisions were coping with something different. We thought we were there to free the Jews but now they turned on us. We were also jumping from one country to another. Persia was having trouble as it was then called, Iran, Iraq, Syria and of course poor old Beirut. We went to Egypt for rest periods for safe areas until their nationalists had a go marching around. We went back to Palestine or the Sinai desert, which I think was the safest place to be. When we formed up again in Jordan and this was an easy place too.

We had to go to Persia as the Russians more or less refused to move. Russia was occupying half of Persia. I thought we were going to have a go at them. We had two battalions of foreign legion and a battalion of Australians and two battalions of UK troops with a tank regiment. So we were a formidable lot. That was including the 24th Guards Brigade which we were in.

There was a compromise dug out and what happened were the Russians agreed to pull out providing the British and French handed over the oil refinery which British Petroleum had built to the Persians, also the pipeline from the end of Iraq and Syria into this oil refinery. After the buzzing and talking they eventually agreed and we then pulled back to Syria. The Syrians then demanded independence from the French. Now we were under the French command up to then. In fact I got a medal from them, but unfortunately things deteriorated some what and when the French army which we were once with started getting tough with the Syrians they made us go in-between the two. They eventually agreed to pull out to Beirut. We pulled out and headed to Beirut or Palestine not quite sure, and the Syrians were left to do their own thing.

This episode concerned the medal for Palestine 1945 to 1948. This is quite interesting medal but unfortunately to get It men that had came straight from action against the Germans for the Jews were now being killed by the Jews. I am talking about the final episode, I wasn't in Palestine when this happened but our squadron of engineers was. They were called when the King David hotel went up in the air to get the people out. The officer that was killed that was shot dead killed some terrorists and wounded some others was from out squadron. In any case they found 6 people alive and 91 dead.

The main thing was we were not moving out of Palestine fast enough, now I am really sorry for the Jews but don't forget Britain went in to the war to help relieve and rescue the Jews especially the ones from Belsen and the other horrible places that the Germans had for getting rid of the Jews. So I don't believe that the few dead when they claim the Arabs went through compares to what we went through in the war. There was a total in the British cemetery 222 soldiers and police. In any case it a bit of state that when you go in to a so called rest area that you are up to your neck again in fighting for survival.

We were standing on the bridge near the YMCA, it was the Allanbury Bridge, and it was built in the First World War when the British and Australians were fighting the Turks. On camels we went up to Damascus, we didn't get too Damascus as the there were trains as Laurence of Arabia had blown them up and there were still bits and pieces everywhere. Laurence of Arabia was held in very high affection by the tribes, I think there was Bedouins there. As soon as our convoy of camels came up, you could feel eyes on you and it was an open desert. Then suddenly we heard "Sayedi ascari" and then there were the Arabs. They were watching us. To make sure we never took any souvenirs, not that I was going to, that was theirs, we wanted to go and see it. It reminded me of when Laurence of Arabia was dancing on top of that carriage. Anyway that was after the war.

If to go back to the end of the last war, the First World War, they had taken notice of what he was saying because all those countries – Iraq, Iran, Jordan, and Syria were made by Laurence of Arabia – well not made by Laurence but he had a big say in what the Arabs were doing and he more or less promised the Arabs to have some sort of say instead of being broken up into American, French and British zones of interest. Perhaps now all this business in that we are now, would not have taken place.

Anyway the next thing, you could see part of the railway, but part of it was gone. I think souvenir hunters had taken it. The next thing was the terrorism not only just there it was all over, The Russians had got out of

Iraq and Iran, and it was called Persia before. The Russians would not move until we had agreed on the oil and the oil, and the refinery was handed over to now either Iran or Iraq where Persia was.

I told you also when on a camel trip to see the sights where Laurence of Arabia blew up trains, we did see the one which was the last one he blew up when he done his victory in front of all the mass Arabs and they included Fisal – of Iraq who was disposed of by the present ruler, and I think he was the cousin of Jordanian king who he also nominated. We saw the Allanbury Bridge, which linked Palestine with Jordan, and we went to Alan?? And saw the royal palace there. We also saw the royal palace at Cairo when members of tank regiments – of the 7th armoured division, occupied it when they arrested King Faruk. This was during the war and they heard his yacht was ready to sail to Italy, which was under the axis powers.

I also saw the two capital ships that came through the canal listing and they were on their way to America after the Italians had put their mines on them, in Alexandria port in Egypt, and I also saw the Goliath battle wagon that was going east to take the place of the capital ship that had been sunk and it had wooden guns on. It was on old target boat, and I think they had done it up to try and confuse the Japs, because everything that went through the canal obviously finished up in the archives of the German, Italians or Japs. There were enough agents in Cairo to see to that.

The Palestine War

In the years following World War II, Britain's position in Palestine gradually worsened. This was caused by a combination of factors, including:

Rapid deterioration due to the incessant attacks by Irgun and Lehi on British officials, armed forces, and strategic installations. This caused severe damage to British morale and prestige, as well as increasing opposition to the mandate in Britain itself, public opinion demanding to "bring the boys home".

World public opinion turned against Britain as a result of the British policy of preventing the Jewish Zionist Holocaust survivors from reaching Palestine, sending them instead to refugee camps in Cyprus, or even back to Germany, as in the case of Exodus 1947.

The costs of maintaining an army of over 100,000 men in Palestine weighed heavily on a British economy suffering from post-war depression, and were another cause for British public opinion to demand an end to the Mandate.

Finally in early 1947 the British Government announced their desire to terminate the Mandate, and passed the responsibility over Palestine to the United Nations.

23 Field Company was the senior engineer company of 1st British Infantry Division. They moved to Palestine in January 1945 under command Major E V Rambush RE. In 1945 the company moved to Egypt for training at the School of Military Engineering at Ismalia and returned to Palestine as the troubles flared up in October. The Company was employed in construction accommodation and security bases as well as security duties. It was indeed a Captain Gillette of 23rd Field Company RE who cut down the bodies of the two unfortunate Intelligence Sergeants in July 1947. He was temporarily blinded when he cut the body of one sergeant from a tree and the body struck a mine placed by the terrorists below the tree. The Grenadier Guards provided the covering infantry. The company remained in Palestine up to the last withdrawal and then moved into Egypt.

Next minute we were on trucks on the way to Syria. Fear that the French were trying to take over some of the colonies that they had before the war. Syria and Beirut were the two places they were trying to take up, and I think Iran. Anyway we were charging around, this was something we didn't think much on. As some of the French had two battalions of the French Foreign legion, don't know if anyone has heard of Barck?? Harbour, they fought there and then let the 8th Army come forward to save their lives. Now we were in between the French and the Syrians. We all went to Indo-china. I was involved in the fight against terrorism in Middle East including Palestine, Iran and Syria.

In Azerbaijan, whilst in the area took place in a Tiger hunt but used a tank. The tiger was a man-eater but the tank missed!

All over the Middle East at this time there was a lot of bad feeling toward occupying armies and sabotage was rife. One morning we were called out to a line of telegraph poles that had been drilled, and explosives and detonators, together with acid, had been place in the holes, these had to be removed very carefully, one sapper from another company had one detonate, and it had taken his hand off.

We were then asked to go to check out Alenby Bridge to make sure that there were no booby traps; this was given the all clear. While we were there we were talking to the Palestinian police who said that if someone wanted to cause maximum damage to the whole of the middle east, all they would have to do, was interfere with the water supply.

We were chasing terrorists. If we caught a terrorist we took them either to Cyprus (that was before they started and when they started the whole Middle East started), one time we could go into Syria through and from Beirut onto Damascus or the British could go anywhere – Iraq and Iran or even into Russia. In fact there was a route into India which they used to bring in through Afghanistan and Pakistan and into the Middle East, and the division that was going home would go that way as well.

Beirut Mayor

When the Army occupies a reasonable size town we always made a military mayor. The military mayor of Beirut was an Australian, a practising Muslim. He was very proud of the fact of his ancestors had come over to Australia with the camels and formed the camel trains under a major ex-British Army who became an Australian. He was the one that formed the big convoys of camels and now the camels that are wild are being imported back to Arabia. These camels came from India; he was in the Indian Army Camel Corps this Major was. He reckoned the best camel drivers were the Afghans of course their descendents now are Australians.

Mind you at this particular time Beirut was one of the finest cities that I have ever been in and I thought it compared with Rome, but what happened after this was we were rushing around from one thing to another we didn't know if we were coming or going and we got eventually into Beirut and then into Palestine, Where the terrorists were getting active. What we trying to do now and they were saying "you are not going home fast enough" and then you had various things that

427

they were doing like king David hotel, mining telephone poles and one night we were patrolling taking out little bottles of acid that were connected to a detonator that were inside the poles. God knows where they were getting it from but I don't think the Americans wanted to stay in the Middle East, and they definitely didn't want us to go to Japan. There was also a nasty rumour that poison experts from Porton Down had deserted, not deserted but joined akanar Which was one of the Jewish organisations and there was an outbreak of poliomitisis, which was man made or not we don't know. A lot of facts were going through and soldiers are not stupid as they can think.

Out of the blue I won some silver coins and when we were on at our camp one day a little Arab used to come in and make things like brooches and stuff. I went and got these silver coins and said to him "Could you make me up a set of necklace, brooch, bracelets and earrings" and he said yes. He everything there in a very small kit, I think it took him about three days to knock this set up. Jeep said "could have some of that that's left over" I said yeah and he got made a bracelet with his wife's name on it. That finished it, I wanted to have made was that most of the 8th Army had a silver 8 or a silver V which was the Arabic symbol of 8 made up. Unfortunately the time we finished we had run out of silver and a couple of days later we were on the move again.

This took place at or near Beirut.

This is Syria. We went to Beirut to Syria, this was at the end of the war and we were not needed in Japan. We went to Persia because the Russians were occupying half it, and there was a fellow called Musocdivc who was going round crying and singing, he was the prime minister. He wanted the British influence out and he wanted the oil consortium, a huge place. The Russians were more or less supporting him. Although there were us and the French Army, waiting for well just waiting, eventually they compromised, they allowed the Persia's and the Iran's to nationalise the oil and the pipelines and the place where they converted it to different petrol's. They gave a date for withdrawal and we gave a date and we went back to Beirut or before we went to Beirut we went to Syria because the pot was starting to boil there as they wanted independence and the French wanted to put over their kind of government again and we were in the middle again. We were trying to stop the Syrians and by this time the Syrians had built up a big army. The Americans had given quite a lot of support and that was that.

We went back to Beirut. The Beirut I knew and the Beirut that is now being pictured on the news is quite a different place. It was the Paris of the east, all the big oil companies were there and we had a big rest camp there run by the Australians. It was a very fine place to have a rest and our next port of call was trouble in Egypt. There was trouble in Palestine so we were going backwards and forwards like no ones business.

One nasty episode in Jerusalem was the birthday parade of the king, King George. We were all done up like dogs dinners they suddenly found shells under the speaking place if they had gone off it would have made a nice little mess. I think of the poor buggers that was on there and all the people passing by.

One nasty episode was of course the King David Hotel, I wasn't there but quite a lot of my mates were and I did know the officer that got killed. He shot some of the terrorists but that doesn't help the young girls that come out from the UK and were there.

That was part of our colonial heritage but we were advertising that it should be split down the middle, no wanted it, the Americans wanted the Jews to take over of course you see what has happened now. We are going back in a small way to partitioning it – half and half. All they had against us was that we were not going home fast enough. I couldn't get home fast enough I don't know about them the silly buggers started following us back. We used to take terrorists to Cyprus on our HMS destroyers – I think it was the Chieftain.

I never visualised how that would go up in the air as well, the terrorist's parties all over the world were more or less talking to each other "you can kick the lion; I think he has had enough". We did have enough but we don't think they should have done things like that to us. Anyway all I had to look forward to was our homecoming, and we all talk about these bloody armies that never went. I never went home – we went to Africa, went through Sicily and Italy, went back and were going to go Japan. Towards the end of Persia which we now know as Iran and Iraq, although there was a nasty war later on, there didn't seem to be very nationalistic they went on about their business and no one bothered them. I never went as far as over the sea but we did go over as far as the border with the Iran and Iraq – which was going to be such a terrible war there.

Middle East the end

When we got back it was the last time our section was together before they started disbanding to go home. Before that we were chasing the terrorists and Russians were slowing getting in, into Iran and Iraq. We were in a brigade that was up there with them for a bit.

One of my main tasks was taking charges out of telephone poles. They had drilled holes in there put a bottle of acid in there with a detonator and some explosives, which they could get out mines. Silly they did it right in the centre, and so it just dropped down. What they should have done was a hole on the side and blows it down. Anyway that is neither here or there now.

All we had to think about now our little 27 groups was going home and getting demobbed. We had a thing in our papers called Python it meant that after 4 or 5 6 years you could go home and be repatriation.

We were now winding up for our demobilisation, both Jimmy and Jeep were in pretty high group; they were 5 or 6 years older than me, although in service I was the highest, my group 27 which was sent back. We went to the NAAFI and the day came for these two to go back to Port Cyrus and we had a night in the NAAFI, there was a raffle and the prize were crates of Stella beer and I won it. We kept two crates for our troop and the rest that went to the lads in there. After wishing them all good well and saying goodbye to everybody and in the morning they got all their stuff and into the truck and off they went to Cyrus and off home. This was in the Sinai desert. After that we went to couple more do's on bridging and then it was my turn to go and I went from Adeira. We went down by train and as usual it was bombarded with stones at different places, and before I went I went down to the place that the Hampshire's, where my father was at before they went to Gallipoli. Then I went off with home with the trains being bombarded with stones as usual with "Brits go home" which I didn't take too personally.

It is just unfortunate that my name is Britt and when I have been examined my family record it stretches back to serving in military back to waterloo and most of them were born in Ireland or in barracks in Ireland because there was a thing at the time to help the Irish over their troubles especially over the famines. 30% of the entire all the regiments had recruits from Ireland and so whether they were in the regulars or the militia or in my case the territorial's. We seem to serve this country very, very well. Most of my ancestors according to their papers, which we got from Kew – this was after the war served in the foot, regiments of the army.

All the ones that were left they gave the staff jobs to do. My job was to look after the Arab employees who done all the cooking, messes, and toilets and things like that. Some of them drove our wagons too. I stuck on that job until my turn came up in 27 groups.

After a few hectic months the call came for me to return to my homeland after an F.F.I at the nearest Medical Centre. We could now see that we were going to go home as they were getting rid of men over 37. My group was 27 we were probably the last group out of Egypt as we had to go to and embarked on a liner called the Empire Ken.

That expression they use on one of the television shows was "King George Orders and we obey over the hills and far away", but the lads there played football in Portsmouth, some of the youngsters from Corpus Christi School, St Johns, Stamshaw, Northern Parade, most of them were either killed or severely wounded in the last war, besides Africa, Pantelleria, Sicily and Italy. Most of the families deserved the medal for staying in Portsmouth who was under bombardment from the Germans as much as we were abroad. All those skills we had learnt were put into practice for the main assault across the channel. We had more landings, more crossing of rivers they had Sunday dinners. Among our most dubious honours was Saturday Night Soldier, D Day Dodger, Anzio Mole and of course Dockie.

On our way back the Empire Ken broke down, she broke down in the Bay of Biscay of all places. Funny to be on a ship and no sound. Once the engines started up again, off home. Then on to the UK, we sailed into the Clyde and it was very efficient on the way they handled us. Mind you they had a lot of time to do this; customs didn't seem to bother much. We came over the side. I will always remember one lad in front of me. He had one of those very small pianos with three legs, we had to lift him on the gangway, I don't know where he got them from and he came ashore.

I more or less had tinned fruit which you could buy more or less easily in Egypt, mostly South African, on the account of meeting my family and seeing my son which I hadn't seen. This was young Alan. We went down to a town in Suffolk or Surrey and they gave us our civilian clothes and out release books and off we went to Portsmouth. There was about four of us. One who was with me in the Territorial's and another one which I later met when I went back to the dockyard. After arriving at the docks in Scotland we boarded the train for the De-mob centre in the UK where I received my civvy suit and Z reserve papers after which I returned to my home and family. Then into the arms of my loving family again, my days as a soldier were over.

Returning Home

I am not saying that I was a good soldier but like the cure of its egg I was good in parts and in parts I was very good. As that brand that they put on me "backroom Lawyer" well when I did come into Civvy Street I became a shop steward as I said before in the Portsmouth dockyards. I certainly learnt a lot, I learnt a lot, and one of them was you don't trust some of the officers, must of the officers were ok but some and I know their names too, were rubbish and we used to call them medal hunters and they did get their own back on some of the lads at Anzio.

I returned home on 18th March 1946 – returns home and I was put on call up. After my overseas leave was finished the Ministry of Pensions who granted me a 30% pension, examined me. I returned to work in the HM Dockyard, Portsmouth and worked as a skilled labourer and later as a rigger.

Discharge Papers

On my last attack of Bronchitis Dr Corbett treated me. A few weeks later, I received a paper warning me to stand by for call- up and how to use my travel pass. I then went to see Dr Corbett, who was still treating me for bronchitis, and I showed him the warning paper and he said it should not apply to me as I had a Disability pension, and he consulted with an ex-army Dr who said he would have a word with records about it. Two weeks later I received my discharge papers 6th September 1951 and on the bottom was ---CEASING TO FUFIL ARMY PHYSICAL REQUIREMENTS PARA 204 – 11 TAR 1936 and also asking me to return my travel documents to Records. If I had not seen Dr Corbett when I did I would have ended up in Korea as my discharge papers were dated 1951.

Fred Britt (in overalls) in Dockyard during the late 70's / early 80's

Background Information

Frederick "Fred" Frank George Britt was born on the 9th August 1920. On 22nd April 1922 John Philip T Britt was born. John was Fred's brother. John passed away in November 1996 survived by is wife Rose and his two children Roy and Leslie survived him.

When he was two Frederick and John's father died, Frederick Waldemar Britt. Frederick Waldemar Britt died 13th December 1922 at 265 Milton road Portsmouth – workhouse 24 years old of 32 Wilson Road, Northend – acetylene burned and welder –, and the inquest held on December 15th 1922 determined that he died from tubercular meningitis.

Frederick Waldemar Britt was the son of John Henry Britt and Ada Mary. John Henry along with his brother Denis had served in the army for over 20 years, and both of them served during the Boer War. John and Denis' father was also in the army – Michael was also in the army, serving in North America, India and Afghanistan.

John Henry Britt, Ada and daughter

Ada Britt was a renowned drinker and often gin bottles were found up the chimney and in other places. After her daughter Dorothy died in childbirth she took in Dorothy's two daughters Pat and Norma, and at one point in her house there 12 people in a two up two down house. She also has a reputation of being not quite truthful.

Irene's wedding to William O'Neill. John and
Ada Britt are in the back row

Irene with brothers Stanley & Fred

9th October 1913. Frederick Waldemar Britt enlists in 2nd Battalion Hampshire Regiment. When he leaves he was an Acting Corporal number 3/3946. His brother Stanley Britt has already joined the 1st Battalion of the Hampshire Regiment. They both served at during the war and both were wounded.

Frederick Waldemar Britt

Stanley Britt was a corporal in the 1st Hampshire Regiment. He was already in the Army when war broke out in August 1914, and was immediately drafted to France, where he took part in the Battle of Mons and the subsequent retreat, and the Battles of the Marne, the Aisne and Ypres.

Stanley Britt

He was wounded and suffered from shell shock and was consequently sent home. On his recovery he was engaged as an instructor in Machine Gunnery at Gosport until his discharge in March 1916 as medically unfit for further service. He holds the Mons star, and the General Service and Victory Medals.

After Frederick Waldemar Britt's death the family then moved in with their maternal Grandparents – George Triggs who had run the Duke of Connaught's Pub in Copenhagen Street, Portsmouth. When George later retired they moved to 32 Wilson Road, Portsmouth.

George Triggs later died on the 19th March 1928. His wife Mary died in 1936. He had an active naval career. George and Mary also had a son called George who after joining the army came back to live with them for a while.

In 1928 Fred and John's mother remarried to Charles Alfred Evans, who was a sailor in the Royal Navy. They had a son together called Charles William Evans, known to friends and family alike as Charlie who was born in 23rd November 1928. He later died in March 1990. Charlie ended up working in the Portsmouth Dockyards and in later life lived with Fred and Iris Britt. He was a very good darts player and liked smoking the pipe. He worked at the dockyards and was a welder. He passed away in 1990.

Charles William Evans was a keen darts member of the Trade Union Club team in later life. He hit two maximums – two 180's in the Trades Super League. When he died the Golden Lion Men's A team wrote this in the local paper "So many qualities in just one man, kind and gentle loyal through and through. But best of all he was someone we knew"

CHARLIE EVANS, a respected and popular member of the Trades Union Club team.

Mary Caroline Triggs had the nickname "Kit" for some reason, and was a bit of a character as you can imagine given the circumstances. She used to "lay out" anyone who died in the area, and was unofficial "slaughter woman" for the neighbours who had raised pigs for food during wartime rationing and beyond. She used to wrestle the pigs and cut their throats and butcher them for the community.

Mary Britt (Evans)

She also used to like a drink in the Mother Shipton pub in Stamshaw, and was very well respected by all. She died in 1968. She took out a life assurance policy for Gramps when he was 19, 1939, which was to cover his funeral in the event he didn't make it home. Some 70 years later this was cashed in and £1000 was paid out.

Fred, Sapper FFG Britt 882003 – Fred Britt eventually ended up in the Royal Engineers, 4th Armoured Brigade, 626-field squadron and then later the 23rd Field Coy, 1st Infantry Division, 24th Guards Brigade. He was in the Royal Engineers from the 30th April 1940 to 18th March 1946. Prior to this he as in the Royal Artillery from 17th March 1938 to 29th April 1940, as part of the Royal Artillery he was in B Company, Duke Of Connaught, 6th Royal Hampshire's, Portsmouth.

Iris Voysey who would later be married to Fred for 66 years was long associated with Wilson Road as her Grandparents George and Annie lived at 45 Wilson Road, and they had 12 children altogether, 6 boys and 6 girls. Many of their children later lived on the same road.

George and Annie spent the first few years of their married life in Havant Road,

North End, but then moved to 45, Wilson Road, Stamshaw, a rented house which was to remain in the family for many years. It was a small terraced house, with the usual outside toilet in the tiny back garden. There was a small kitchen with a copper bath in which all the washing was done every Monday, a small living-room, and the front sitting-room, which was normally kept tidy for visitors and special occasions, but sometimes had to be used as a spare bedroom. There were three bedrooms upstairs. The six girls slept in one, and the six boys in another. None of the girls went into service, and they didn't marry very young, so the house must have been very crowded when they were growing up.

The children were called George, Anne, Elsie, Albert, Nell, John, Henry, Winifred, Frederick, Reginald, Doris, and Daisy.

The children went to Stamshaw School, where they had a reasonably good elementary education till they were 13 or 14. When they left, some of the girls went to work in the local corset factory. Elsie worked in a lemonade factory, while Winnie remained at home to help her mother. Gradually they all got married, except for Fred, who remained at home. Winnie also remained there, with her husband and later two sons.

Several of the children settled near their old home, and at one time there were four Voysey households in Wilson Road, and another four within a short walk.

George died in 1937, but Annie lived on till 1953. During the years after the war, up till her death, it was the custom to have a big family party at her house every Christmas Day, starting with tea for the children at about 4 o'clock, and going on till the early hours of Boxing Day.

George Voysey Sr, Nelly & Annie Voysey

The eldest boy, George was born in 1897. He fought in France during the First World War, and married Mabel. Their children were Roy, Iris (later Fred's wife), Doreen and Brenda. They lived at 14 Wilson Road for many years.

Mabel & George Voysey

George & Mabel with daughters

Voysey family with extended family including Britts

Roy with Brenda, Doreen and Iris

Anne, the eldest girl, born 1899, often called by the nickname Dinah. She married Donald Walters, from the West Indies, but they had no children. They had a chicken farm at Cowplain before the war, with a real gypsy caravan and a large hut for living accommodation. During the blitz many members of the family stayed out there to avoid the bombing, and after the war they kept the land on for several years and it was used for family picnics.

Elsie, born 1900, married Frederick Charles Bealing, who was in the Navy and travelled to many countries including China. Their first child, a boy, only lived a few days.

They then had three girls, Joan, Doris and Margaret, but Joan died of blood poisoning at the age of 7. Then Frederick died on HMS Royal Oak in 1939. After moving around several times because of the war, she eventually settled in 10,Wilson Road for the rest of her life. She died suddenly of a stroke when she was only in her early sixties

Life after war

> In reply please
> quote: AE/50
> Date: **10 MAR 1947**
>
> RE Record Office,
> Ditchling Road,
> Brighton
>
> Sir,
>
> 1. With reference to your claim for Campaign Stars and Medals, I have to inform you that the following has/have been verified and approved :-
>
> 1939/45 Star ✓
> African Star ✓
> ~~Pacific Star~~
> ~~Burma Star~~
> Italy Star ✓
> ~~France — Germany Star~~
> ~~Atlantic Star~~
> Defence Medal ✓
>
> 2. No claim is required for the War Medal 1939/45. ✓
>
> 3. The date on which Campaign Stars and Medals will be available for issue by this office is uncertain, but an announcement will be made, in due course, by the BBC and the National Press.
>
> Mr F F G BRITT
> 32 LION TERRACE
> PORTSEA PORTSMOUTH
>
> I am, Sir, Your obedient Servant,
>
> Colonel i/c RE Records

> **MINISTRY OF PENSIONS**
> ~~NORCROSS~~
> ~~BLACKPOOL~~
> ~~LANCS.~~
> CHELTENHAM,
> GLOS.
>
> Sir,
>
> The Minister of Pensions is commanded by His Majesty the King to forward to you the King's Badge for members of the Armed Forces, the Merchant Navy, the Home Guard and the Civil Defence Organisations who are disabled as a result of war service.
>
> I am, Sir,
> Your obedient Servant,
>
> H. Parker
> Secretary.
>
> Mr F F G Britt

Fred Britt was awarded the following medals: -

- The 1939 - 45 Star was granted for service in operations between 3rd September 1939 and 15th August 1945, the date on which active operations against Japan ceased in the Pacific. The qualifying period for the Army was 6 months in an operational command not based in the UK.
- The Africa Star was awarded to the armed forces for entry into an operational area in North Africa between 10th June 1940 (the date of Italy's entry into the war) and 12th May 1943 (the end of operations in North Africa). Silver 1 or 8 worn on the ribbon indicates service with the 1st or 8th Army.
- The Italy Star was granted to those on operational service in Italy, Sicily and countries bordering the Aegean Sea at any time between the capture of Pantallerio on 11th June 1943 and VE (Victory Europe) Day 8th May 1945.
- The Defence Medal was granted for 3 years service at home or 6 months

overseas. In the case of bomb disposal units, or mine the time qualification was 3 months. Service to qualify for the award counted from 3rd September 1939 to 8th May 1945 in Great Britain; and to forces overseas until the end of active hostilities in the Pacific 15th August 1945.
- War Medal, 1939 -45 awarded to full time personnel of the armed forces wherever they served; qualification being 28 days service. Period covered by service 3rd September 1939 to 2nd September 1945.
- Efficiency Medal
- GS Medal with clasp Palestine
- He was awarded the Kings Badge – disabled as a result of war service.

Rank on discharge – sapper and he left ceasing to fulfil army physical requirements Para 204 – 11 – TAR 1936. Height 5'10" blue eyes, fair hair

Testimonial of Sapper Britt on release - "Sapper Britt has been with the unit about two years. He is a good steady worker, who given a job will see it through to the finish.

460

He is trustworthy and thoroughly honest" – 15th March 1946 signed by Major RE.

On the 18th June 1946 he restarted work back in the dockyards as a labourer, two days after returning home.

On the 6th September 1951 he was discharged from being on call up. He had exemplary conduct and was discharged at Brighton. He had service with colours 6 years 291 days, service on class reserve 5 years 80 days and a total service of 13 years 174 days

1952 to 1956 – joined 21st Battalion Hampshire Regiment (Portsmouth and Dockyards), as part of the home guard. As part of his job he was part of a sabotage squad to stop the Russians after a nuclear attack in Portsmouth. Part of his training would be to hide out in the tunnels around Portsmouth in the event of an attack. He was a corporal whilst in this battalion. Afterwards he received a letter which read as follows:-

"I wish to express my sincere appreciation of the loyal and willing service which you gave to the Country as an active member of the Home Guard during the period of 1952 – 1956". Anthony Head, Secretary of State of War.

10th July 1956 – appointed established skilled labourer at Portsmouth yard. As part of working in the dockyard he also did further training in such courses as "How to be a student", "Payment by results", and "Work study for Trade Unionists".

12th August 1981 – Imperial Service Medal in recognition of long and meritorious service

PORT ADMIRAL PORTSMOUTH
HM Naval Base Portsmouth PO1 3LE

Telephone 0705 (Portsmouth) 22351 ext 22001/23063

F. F. G. Britt, Esq
24 Stratfield Gardens
HAVANT
PO9 4LS

Your reference
Our reference 422/5/81
Date 6 April 81

Dear Mr Britt

The Port Admiral has asked me to inform you that Her Majesty the Queen has been graciously pleased to award you the Imperial Service Medal in recognition of long and meritorious service.

Your medal and certificate are being prepared and arrangements will then be made for the Port Admiral to present the medal to recipients at a simple ceremony. I will write to you again as soon as final arrangements have been made.

Yours sincerely

SECRETARY TO
PORT ADMIRAL PORTSMOUTH

He and his brother Charlie helped in the preparation of Task Force for the Falkland Island Operation during April to June 1982. He was also a shop steward of the T&GWU. He was also the chair of the 2/92 Portsmouth Naval Base Branch – Fleet Maintenance and repair organisation for 10 years.

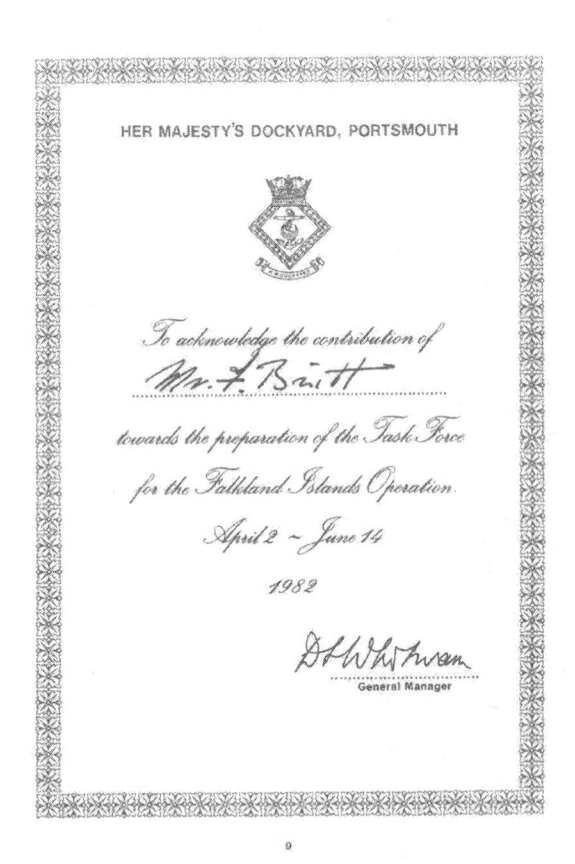

He always renewed his passport, and although he travelled far and wide as part of his effort during the war he never used it.

TRANSPORT AND GENERAL WORKERS' UNION

Regional Secretary: J. C. ASHMAN

Regional Office: Transport House, 67/75 London Road, Southampton SO9 5HH
Telephone: Southampton 23426/7 23179 Telex: 47425

REGION No. 2

Regional Secretary: J. C. ASHMAN
Registered Offices: Transport House, Smith Square, London SW1. Telegraphic Address: "Transunion, Sowest, London". Tel: 01-828-7788

Your Ref: Our Ref: A/H/P/B.182(b) When replying please quote reference

Bro. F. Britt, 23rd September 1982
2/22 Branch

Dear Brother Britt,

<u>Union Recognition – Regional Statuette</u>

I am pleased to inform you that the Regional Finance and General Purposes Committee in session on the 20th September discussed in full the services you personally have afforded to this Union and its members over many years.

Accordingly, they unanimously agreed, in appreciation of your valuable and sterling work, to award you the Union's Regional Statuette and Certificate of Merit.

Furthermore they requested that I extend to you their very best wishes for the future and I take pleasure in associating myself with this expression of goodwill.

Best wishes and kind regards.

Yours sincerely,

John Ashman
Regional Secretary

General Secretary: A. M. EVANS Deputy General Secretary: A. KITSON

Termination of service – dockyards official secrets act signed 11/8/82 – service number 2687535 Rank / grade S/L

Medal award from Federation des combatants allies en Europe – association nationale des resistants – Croix allies 1992 (allied cross) FCAEE.

Fred and Iris celebrated their 60th Wedding Anniversary in 2001.

I am so pleased to know that you are celebrating your Diamond Wedding anniversary on 27th September, 2001. I send my congratulations and best wishes to you on such a special occasion.

Elizabeth R

Mr. and Mrs. Frederick Britt

test of time

Couple shared a street and have gone on to share 60 happy years together

by Catherine Burt
The News

DIAMOND wedding couple Iris and Fred Britt met when out with friends having never realised they lived in the same street.

The pair, then both from Wilson Road, Stamshaw, fell in love and were married in 1941 at the Corpus Christi Roman Catholic Church in Gladys Avenue, North End.

Mrs Britt, 77, said: 'We had never met until we were further away with friends and it was a shock to find out we both lived in the same road.'

Sixty years on, the couple, who live in Stratfield Gardens, Warren Park, celebrated their diamond wedding anniversary at a surprise party, held in Leigh Park Working Men's club in Dunsbury Way.

Mr Britt – who saw army service in Africa and the Middle East – was a shop steward at Portsmouth dockyard and Mrs Britt worked in a corset factory.

Mr Britt, 81, said: 'We were some of the first people to move up to Leigh Park and this is where we have settled.'

The couple enjoy going on holidays with the over-50s clubs in Havant and Leigh Park.

Mrs Britt said: 'We are quite happy and we have all our family, even if they don't all live close to us.'

The couple have four children, 13 grand-children and 12 great-grand-children.

Iris and Fred Britt marked 60 years of marriage with a surprise party

Iris and Fred back in 1941

Fred and Iris were married for 66 years. They had four children – Alan, Iris, Carole, and John. They also fostered several children such as Julian and Moira. They did have a dog called Lucky, who was a puppy that next door, Mrs "Dora" Purrington's dog had. She was Diane's Mum, who in turn was Julian's Mum, one of Nanny and Grampy's foster children. They also did look after a young girl for a couple of years who's Mum had had a breakdown of some sort, whose name was Moira. It was quite an informal arrangement back in the 50's. Nan said that she only got involved in it as the neighbour, again Mrs Purrington, did it first, and Nan and Gramps saw what a rewarding thing it was to do for these poor kids, plus they did get a small allowance for doing it, nothing like the fortune that is paid today for professional foster parents!

They had a happy life and although Fred was awarded a total of ten medals he once wrote a photo taken of his four children and wife – "My Real Medals".

"my real medals"

Iris, Iris and Carole

Iris, Fred and Carole

Britt's in the Garden

Iris, Iris, Carole & Alan

The Britt family in the 1960's

Back row - Alan, Fred

Middle Row - Mary, Iris, George Voysey, Iris (wife)

Front row - John, Carole

Fred with children

Carole and Iris

Alan married three times to Janet, Pat and Darlene. He has a total of five children – David, Elaine, Roger, Julie and Vincent.

Iris married Graham and they have three children – Joanne, Sasha, and Adam.

Carole married Kevin Simmons and they have three children – Colin, Kate, and Christopher. Colin marries Helen Woolston and they have two children, Bethany and William.

John marries Angela, and they have three children – James, Daniel and Laura.

A number of the grandchildren have since had children of their own.

Grampy passed away on the 1st November 2007, his wife, my Nan, passed away 10 months later on the 23rd September 2008, closely followed by my Mother, Carole, their daughter on the 30th September.

I miss them all, but this book has allowed me to put together one final story from Grampy. What follows next is my last conversation with Grampy, I hope this does you proud Gramps.

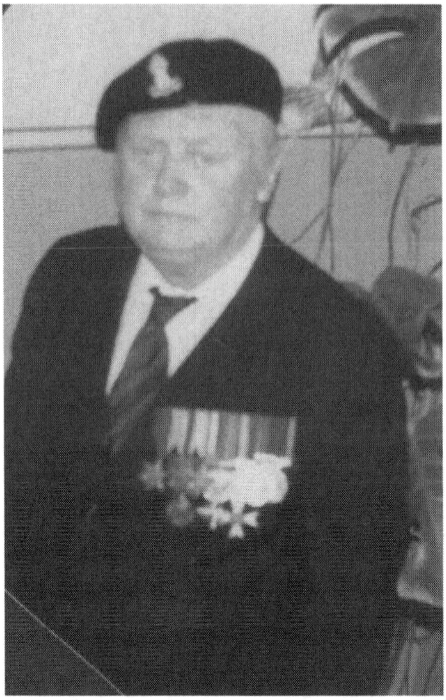

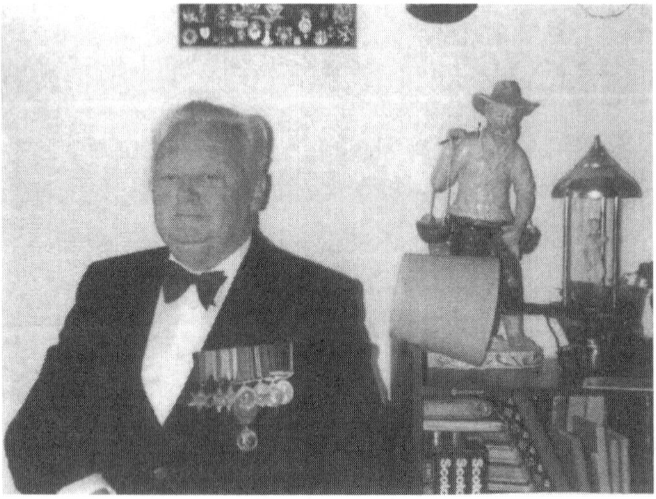

Speech at his funeral – 13th November 2007

As his loving grandson, I have the honour to speak here today on your behalf and on behalf of our family.

My grandfather, Grampy, Frederick Britt, was a war hero from a line of heroes. His father, his grandfathers, his great grandfathers all served in the military, and fought in some of the most important battles this country has been involved in.

Fred Britt was born in August 1920. He was the son of Frederick and Mary Britt. He had a brother John, who was two years younger than him. Back then the world was a different place; it was a country that had just survived one world war and financial hardship. His own father was wounded and had survived Gallipoli.

When Fred was two his father tragically died, and he went to live with his maternal grandfather George Triggs who ran the Duke of Connaught's Pub in Copenhagen Street, Portsmouth. George Triggs had a profound influence on Gramps and taught him about what it was to be a grandfather. They often went on long walks round Portsmouth together talking about the past and the large extended family Grampy had.

Later his mother remarried to Charles Evans and they had a son called Charlie. As Fred turned 15 he left school and took an apprenticeship at Pitt and Sons, local builders. After 18 months being stuck in the cold and damp so he took a job at Streten Brothers And Tanner Ltd, this was a dairy. Working there was his future father in law – George Voysey. At the dairy was a nasty gang of individuals but Gramps unlike his friends wasn't scared. He went up to them and said, "if you start it I will finish it". He never got any trouble after that.

When he turned 17 he did three things, which would stay with him for the rest of his life. Firstly he joined the Territorial Army as part of the 6th Duke of Connaught's Own Battalion, Hampshire Regiment. Secondly he started work at the dockyards and most importantly he met Iris Voysey.

As part of his work with the TA's he took part in the King George VI coronation parade in Portsmouth, and as part of team was awarded the King's Cup for Coast defence Gunners for their accuracy in a competition.

With the outbreak of the war he was stationed at No Mans Fort in the Solent and also at Southsea. During 1940 he passed an intelligence test, by as he put it making sure he never said anything. He then began his training as a Royal Engineer. Whilst in training he first met Denis Healey –who would later be his commanding officer. He made it to the rank of Corporal, which he would later resign as it more work than it was worth!

Before he left the UK he married Iris in September 1941 and in the early part of 1942 was sent to Africa as part of the 8th Army. He quickly got the nickname as the "booby trap king" for his skills with mines and explosives. He saw action in Africa and Italy and he took part in many major battles including the battle of El Alamein, invasion of Pantallerio, the invasion of Italy and the battle of Anzio.

He worked alongside Popski's private army and also helped disarm a bomb, which was found on a boat full of petrol. He had to regularly lay mines, which was an extremely dangerous job, and also he was part of a team that tunnelled under the Germans during the conflict in Italy. In the desert he was often tasked with finding water and also building bridges for the armoured brigade he was attached to.

He met the Pope – Pope Pius XII during the liberation of Rome and he also carved his name in some famous monuments such as the Coliseum in Rome and the Great Pyramid in Egypt

Grampy developed an excellent sideline during the war in that he would often acquire hand grenades and other weapons, which he would deactivate and sell to the yanks and officers.

After the war had finished in Europe he hoped to go home but instead he was sent to take part in the Palestine War. He went to Iran and Iraq and travelled far in the Middle East. During this conflict he went tiger hunting in a tank – he missed! Grampy never considered himself to be a good soldier but as he once said " I was good in parts and in parts I was very good".

I once asked Grampy what he thought of the Germans now and he said that he wasn't bothered by them and didn't hate them. That was typical Grampy always saw the good in everyone and bore no malice.

He had a healthy disregard for officers though, who he didn't trust-he termed them as either rubbish or medal hunters. A couple of times he was charged with conduct prejudious to good order and military discipline, whilst having heated discussions with his superiors on the finer points of warfare. He always stood his ground and he was always right. It was this reputation, which gave him his second nickname – the back room lawyer.

The skills, which he gained as the back room lawyer, helped him when he entered Civvy Street to be a shop steward back at Portsmouth Dockyards. Where he then worked for the next 30 years. In his time there he saw the Mary Rose come into harbour and also worked on the Victory.

In 1952 he was called up to be part of the home guard and was part of the 21st Battalion Hampshire Regiment (Portsmouth and Dockyards). This was set up to be a sabotage squad to stop the Russians after a nuclear attack in Portsmouth.

Over the years Grampy and Nan had 4 children (Alan, Iris, Carole, and John) 15 grand children, 15 great grand children and one great great grandchild. When you add in partners it creates one big crowd. To help remember names Grampy renamed everyone so we were all called Gungadin.

Eventually Nan and Grampy settled at Stratfield Gardens, at Warren Park. It was here they also let stay Pop – Grampy's father in law, Charlie his brother, various foster children, and also when needed various grandchildren when our parents wanted to have some time for themselves! That was typical of the Britt household as everyone was welcome at that house.

He would often have competitions with his brother Charlie to see who had the biggest stomach. He was a regular at Leigh Park Social Club and also the Royal British Legion. He often won so many raffles that we often thought he most be fencing stolen goods! In true Gramps style, he often gave away what he had won to friends and family.

He loved antiques and would often spend many an hour at car boots trying to find that next bargain that would be worth a fortune. He also liked to watch warfare programs to learn from our mistakes.

He regularly took photos, and his photo albums are quite random. I once asked him why he would put photos from the 1960s next to a photo from today next to a photo from the war. He replied it was to make people think. Typical Gramps.

We may no longer see him but we'll always have these special moments we shared with him. When I think of Gramps I think of the words of Rudyard Kipling when he said, "you are a better man than me Gungadin".

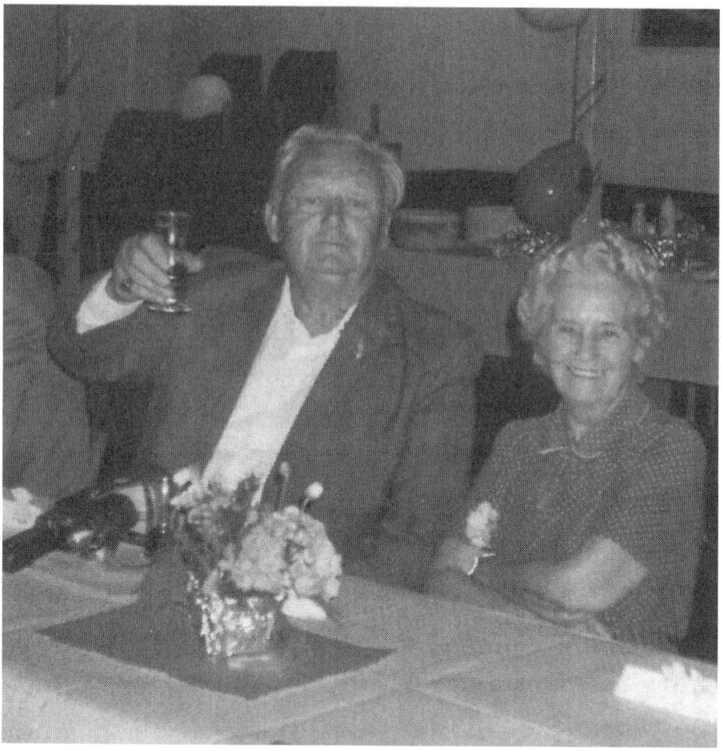